Home Office Research Study 206

The criminal histories of serious traffic offenders

Gerry Rose

Research, Development and Statistics Directorate
Home Office

Home Office Research Studies

The Home Office Research Studies are reports on research undertaken by or on behalf of the Home Office. They cover the range of subjects for which the Home Secretary has responsibility. Titles in the series are listed at the back of this report (copies are available from the address on the back cover). Other publications produced by the Research, Development and Statistics Directorate include Research Findings, the Research Bulletin, Statistical Bulletins and Statistical Papers.

The Research, Development and Statistics Directorate

RDS is part of the Home Office. The Home Office's purpose is to build a safe, just and tolerant society in which the rights and responsibilities of individuals, families and communities are properly balanced and the protection and security of the public are maintained.

RDS is also a part of the Government Statistical Service (GSS). One of the GSS aims is to inform Parliament and the citizen about the state of the nation and provide a window on the work and performance of government, allowing the impact of government policies and actions to be assessed.

Therefore -

Research Development and Statistics Directorate exists to improve policy making, decision taking and practice in support of the Home Office purpose and aims, to provide the public and Parliament with information necessary for informed debate and to publish information for future use.

"The views expressed in this report are those of the authors, not necessarily those of the Home Office (nor do they reflect Government policy)."

First published 2000

Application for reproduction should be made to the Communications and Development Unit, Room 201, Home Office, 50 Queen Anne's Gate, London SW1H 9AT.

© Crown copyright 2000   ISBN 1 84082 517 0

ISSN 0072 6435

Foreword

This report examines the extent to which anti-social behaviour on the road is linked to other criminal activity. Are those who commit serious traffic offences normally law-abiding or are they likely to be involved in other types of crime?

The study examined three types of serious traffic offender – the drink driver, the disqualified driver and the dangerous driver – and revealed that many offenders from each group had committed mainstream offences (violence against the person, burglary, robbery, theft and handling, criminal damage, drug offences). There were significant differences between the groups in terms of their socio-demographic profile and frequency of offending. Disqualified drivers, for example, had criminal histories and an age-profile similar to that of mainstream offenders. Drink drivers were often older and were less involved in other offending, although they were still twice as likely as the general population to have a criminal conviction. Serious traffic offending is predominantly a male activity, and relatively few females are involved.

These findings highlight the potential to disrupt mainstream crime through targeting serious traffic offenders. As such, the report provides a useful basis for further developing an intelligence-led approach to road policing.

Carole F Willis
Head of Policing and Reducing Crime Unit
Research, Development and Statistics Directorate
Home Office
November 2000

Acknowledgements

I wish to thank my colleagues at the Institute of Criminology, Anthony Bottoms, Janet Foster and Ben Bowling for their encouragement, advice and support throughout this project. Belinda Brooks-Gordon's work as research assistant for the fieldwork stage was outstanding, and the quality of the interviews with officers owes much to her professionalism. Nadim Karim and Kathryn Curran made valuable early contributions to the literature review.

Within the Home Office Policing and Reducing Crime Unit, I am especially grateful to Rick Brown for his support throughout the project, and to Joanna Sallybanks for invaluable editorial advice. The analysis of Offenders Index data would not have been possible without the generous help and advice of Chris Kershaw of the Home Office Research, Development and Statistics Directorate.

Stage 2 of the project involved fieldwork with three police forces. In each force the guidance of senior officers was invaluable, and in particular I would like to thank Mark Custerson, Martin McKenna, John Bond, Nigel Short, Ian Bell, Peter Stas and Brian Horrocks. This part of the research would not have been possible without the help of the officers who gave so freely of their time for interviews.

The Author

Gerry Rose is a Senior Research Fellow at the Institute of Criminology, University of Cambridge.

PRC would like to thank Professor Roy Carr-Hill of the University of York for acting as independent assessor for this report.

Contents

List of tables

List of figures

Executive summary

This report was commissioned to gain further understanding of the contribution of road policing to dealing with crime and anti-social behaviour generally. It examines the extent to which anti-social behaviour on the road is linked to criminal activity by assessing whether those who commit serious traffic offences are normally law-abiding members of the public or whether they are likely to have committed other types of criminal offence.

Methodology

The socio-demographic characteristics and the criminal histories of serious traffic offenders were examined using two existing data sources: the Home Office's Offenders Index (OI) and a national survey of Young People and Crime (YPAC). Three main types of serious traffic offending were studied – drink driving, disqualified driving and dangerous driving – and compared to mainstream criminal offending. Mainstream criminal offending in the context of this report included violence against the person, burglary, robbery, theft and handling stolen goods (not involving motor vehicles), criminal damage and drug offences. Interviews were also carried out in three police forces in order to investigate how serious traffic incidents were policed.

Profile of serious traffic offenders

The socio-demographic profile of serious traffic offenders can be summarised as:

- Serious traffic offending was found to be mainly a *male* activity. Females made up only 8 per cent of drink drivers, less than 3 per cent of disqualified drivers and less than 5 per cent of dangerous drivers. Among mainstream offenders, 13 per cent were female.

- Serious traffic offenders were of a similar age profile to mainstream offenders with the exception of drink drivers, many of whom were older (48% of the OI sample were aged over 33). For disqualified drivers, dangerous drivers, and mainstream offenders, between 60 per cent and 75 per cent of convicted offenders were in the age-range 18 to 32.

- The prevalence of traffic offending was higher for young white people than for those from other ethnic groups.

- Young males from higher socio-economic (SES) groups were significantly more likely to commit drink driving offences, whereas young males from lower SES groups were marginally more likely to commit licence and insurance offences.

Offending patterns of serious traffic offenders

Analysis of criminal histories from the OI concentrated on the links between serious traffic offending, 'mainstream' criminal offending and vehicle theft. The analysis examined current court convictions, past offending behaviour and reconvictions. Clear differences were found between the three serious traffic offender groups, especially in comparison with mainstream offenders.

- **Drink drivers** were about twice as likely to have previous convictions as would be expected in the general population. Although 40 per cent of drink drivers had a criminal history, this was less extensive than any other group of offenders examined in this study and the average time since a last conviction was eight years. Drink drivers usually appeared in court for only that offence, rather than a number of offences (as was the case with other offender groups). Drink driving was not closely associated with criminal offending.

- **Disqualified drivers** had criminal histories similar to those of mainstream offenders (79% had a criminal record as compared with 72% of mainstream offenders). They had a similar number of previous convictions, and their likelihood of subsequent conviction within a year was the same (at 37%). The reconviction patterns of this group showed some tendency to repeat disqualified driving but within a more generalised context of offending.

- **Dangerous drivers**[1] showed less involvement with crime than disqualified drivers but more than drink drivers. Approximately 50 per cent had a previous conviction and a quarter was reconvicted within a year. The research suggested there may be two groups of dangerous drivers: about a third had previous convictions that included car theft, and were otherwise similar to recidivist mainstream offenders and disqualified drivers; the other two-thirds showed criminal histories more similar to those of drink drivers.

---

1   Including a small number convicted of causing death by dangerous driving.

The YPAC survey data supported the findings from the OI, especially on the association between mainstream offending and serious traffic offending.[2]

Policing traffic incidents

Interviews were carried out with 132 officers in three forces to find out the way in which traffic incidents were policed; the interviews focused on four offence types — drink driving, disqualified driving, dangerous driving and criminal offences arising from traffic incidents. Traffic officers dealt with serious traffic incidents on a regular basis but not necessarily daily or even weekly. For example, on average four months had elapsed since last dealing with a drink driving incident and 14 months since the last dangerous driving incident. In 62 per cent of cases, the incidents involved two or more offences; however, this varied depending on the main offence type. For example, 75 per cent of disqualified driving incidents involved more than one offence in comparison to only 41 per cent of drink driving incidents. Minor traffic offences were the most common secondary offence for all offence groups; nearly 20 per cent of disqualified driving and dangerous driving incidents involved further serious traffic offences, and 15 per cent involved mainstream crime. In over half the crime incidents, the offences were not traffic or vehicle related, but were mainstream crimes (including drug offences).

About half of disqualified driving and drink driving cases were identified through routine patrol and stops, although in the former prior information or intelligence was a key factor, and in the latter observation and offender behaviour were the key to discovering the offence. Dangerous driving incidents and crime incidents, however, were identified through a number of ways including attending an accident, directly observed in action, reported and radioed through for action and complaints from the public.

The incidents also showed that most offenders had travelled only short distances from home when committing offences, and this was true across all offence groups.

---

2   The YPAC survey also showed that for females, drug use and mainstream offending were equally closely associated with serious traffic offending; for males, the association with drug use was less important.

Implications

This report highlights the significant role that road policing can have in both the enforcement of traffic offences and in combating mainstream crime. A number of implications have been drawn from this study:

- The findings can be used to profile (albeit rather crudely) serious traffic offenders which could guide and focus effort when devising strategies to target offenders and offending behaviour through specific initiatives. The low incidence of females and young black males committing serious traffic offences should be taken into consideration when targeting offenders.

- Targeting repeat serious traffic offenders could be used as a tool to help disrupt mainstream crime as certain groups of these offenders are also likely to commit mainstream offences.

- Analysis of the criminal careers of minor traffic offenders could provide information regarding links with serious traffic offending and mainstream offending. The most likely connections are with traffic offences that involve dishonesty.

- A more sensitive profile of serious traffic offenders could be developed following re-analysis of the OI data in the future when there will be a more extensive data source including serious traffic offences.

- Traffic officers have a dual role in the detection of both traffic offences and mainstream crime. This role should be enhanced further due to the contribution that can be made in the gathering of general intelligence.

- Intelligence could be used to a greater degree in the enforcement of disqualified driving. There is a very close association between disqualified driving and other kinds of offending and this link should be exploited.

- The flow of intelligence between traffic officers and other uniform/CID officers could be improved and local intelligence officers could contribute significantly to this through liaison and co-ordination.

- Data quality is crucial to the role of traffic officers and improvements to links and accessibility of data sources such as PNC and DVLA could be considered.

1.   Introduction

Background

This study was commissioned to complement research previously carried out by the Policing and Reducing Crime Unit (PRCU). A study investigating road policing activity (Ogilvie-Smith et al, 1994) found that 30 per cent of a traffic officer's time was spent dealing with traffic incidents and checks; about 25 per cent of time was devoted to preventative patrol, covering both traffic and crime, and a further 7 per cent was spent on individual crime incidents. Since the early 1990s, the objectives and the organisational structure of road policing have been the subject to much rethinking, especially in relation to crime work. A 1996 Association of Chief Police Officers (ACPO) survey mentioned 29 forces with specific initiatives targeting crime through intelligence-led road policing (ACPO, 1997). The importance of road policing for crime work has also been widely acknowledged by senior officers, for example:

> "A criminal can rob a bank in Carlisle and be back in London in a few hours. My own traffic officers arrest more persons for crime than did my CID" (Joslin, 1994).

> "Most drivers are not criminals but most criminals are drivers ... Routine traffic duties often bring officers into contact with such criminals and traffic patrols continued to make crime a priority during the year – 36 per cent of all arrests made by traffic officers were for crime." (West Midlands Police, Traffic Division, 1997).

The National Road Policing Strategy (ACPO, 1998) stated the strategic aim of road policing to be 'To secure an environment where the individual can use the roads with confidence, free from death, injury, damage or fear'. One of the key objectives of this strategy is to bring about a reduction in road user related crime, to be achieved through intelligence-led targeted enforcement and education of both vulnerable groups and offenders. The changing role of road policing has been emphasised by Government, ACPO and HMIC as an "integral part of core policing" (HMIC, 1998).

Previous research

Criminal histories

In the context of this report, a 'criminal history' refers to the cumulative record of court appearances of an individual (see also Home Office, 1998a). In a comprehensive review, Farrington (1994) defined a criminal career as "... the longitudinal sequence of offences committed by an individual offender". Much of the framework developed for studies of criminal careers, such as the onset and frequency of offending, specialisation in types of offence, the incidence and prevalence of offending within a given period, is used in this study.

Specialisation in offending is a crucially important issue since it probes the connections between serious traffic offending and convictions for other types of offence. In general, the emphasis in criminal career research has been on 'mainstream' offending as a whole, rather than on particular types of offence. Farrington's conclusions on specialisation were that "... there is a small degree of specificity superimposed on a great degree of generality or versatility in offending"; within this framework, the two offence types noted as showing the highest levels of specialisation were sex offending and fraud (1994:535). Blumstein et al (1986) came to a similar conclusion regarding specialisation and found the most specialised offence types for US adults to be drugs and fraud.

Given these findings, two important points can be made:

- Studies of criminal careers have focused on mainstream crime, and have taken no account of serious traffic offending.
- Where there is evidence of specialisation in particular types of offence, it is superimposed on more general and diverse patterns of offending.

We should also note that previous research has concentrated mainly on males, although it is clear that there are differences between the criminal careers of males and females.

Serious traffic offenders

Very few studies have dealt directly with the criminal histories of serious traffic offenders. Recent research has been concerned with issues such as driver education, deterring the drinking driver, and the effects of alcohol and drug use on accident risk. Only rarely have these studies involved any collection of data on mainstream offending, so links to criminal histories have not been made.

Willett (1964) undertook a detailed study of those convicted of six motoring offences: causing death by dangerous driving; driving recklessly or dangerously; driving under the influence of drink or drugs; failing to stop after, or report, an accident; failing to insure against third party risks; and driving while disqualified.[3] Twenty-three percent of the sample had a police record for non-motoring offences, and Willett concluded that serious motoring offenders, contrary to popular belief, were not a random cross section of the motoring population. They were most often (i) young males, (ii) probably motor-cyclists, (iii) in manual occupations, and (iv) more criminal, in terms of previous convictions, than the population as a whole. Wolf (1964) came to similar conclusions about Danish motoring offenders.

In Willett's research, traffic offenders were regarded as a fairly homogeneous group. An important refinement (largely based on a re-analysis of Willett's data) was introduced by Steer and Carr-Hill (1967) who divided traffic offenders into two main groups: 'driving offenders' and 'dishonest offenders'.

- Dishonest offenders (convicted of failing to insure against third party risks or driving while disqualified) exhibited the four characteristics that Willett attributed to serious motoring offenders in general.

- Driving offenders (convicted of causing death by dangerous driving, reckless driving, drunken driving, or failing to stop after an accident), by contrast, seemed to live up to the popular stereotype of motoring offenders; they were a fair cross-section of the motoring population, and could be regarded as average motorists.[4]

Although Steer and Carr-Hill suggested that driving offenders might be no more criminal than the average motorist, their assessment was hampered by a lack of available criminal conviction data for the general population. Whilst this analysis stems from the 1960s, it is relevant to the present study in suggesting important ideas about distinctions between groups of traffic offenders that will be pursued in this report.[5]

---

3   Willett's sample was 653 offenders, convicted in one Home County.
4   An almost identical division was made by Macmillan (1975) ('moving offenders' versus 'dishonest offenders'); Dix and Layzell (1983), within a more detailed typology, distinguished between offences committed consciously and those committed unconsciously.
5   It should also be borne in mind that car ownership levels have increased over the last thirty years from 31% of households owning one or more cars in 1961 to 70% in 1998. By 1998, 79% of adults aged 21-50 held full driving licences (representing 86% of males and 72% of females in this age group) (ONS, 2000). These trends may have an effect on the propensity of offending, in that there is greater opportunity for more individuals to commit traffic offences today than there was in the 1960s, when Willett and Steer and Carr-Hill carried out their studies.

More recent studies on traffic offenders include:

- Riley (1985) explored drink drivers' perceptions of their offending behaviour and the consequent legal penalties. He showed that those reporting drink-driving admitted to significantly higher rates of criminal offending than 'non-drink-drivers' (1985: Table 5).

- Mirrlees-Black (1993) outlined the factors associated with compliance with disqualification: forfeiture of own vehicle; awareness of the potential penalties for driving whilst disqualified; a belief that police monitor disqualified drivers; and the family having a restraining influence.

- Smerdon and South (1997) found that individuals who are determined to drive develop a range of strategies to avoid detection for driving without insurance. If caught and disqualified, many will continue to drive. This was predominantly a male phenomenon, and was found to be bound up with 'car culture'.

- Sugg's (1998) study of offenders attending 'motor projects' run by probation services gave more explicit attention to criminal histories. Most of the offenders were convicted for vehicle taking, but a small group had failed to comply with disqualification. The results showed that the motoring offenders were not specialists but had previous convictions for theft (75%), burglary (60%) and offences of violence against the person (30%). Reconvictions (over a two year period) were most frequently for driving whilst disqualified (49%) or driving without insurance (48%); however, non-motoring offences were also common, for example theft (39%), burglary (25%) and violence against the person (15%).

- Chenery et al (1999) showed evidence of offender targeting through monitoring illegal parking in disabled bays. The study showed that one in five vehicles illegally parked in a disabled space would warrant immediate police action in comparison to 2 per cent of legally parked vehicles. One in three keepers of vehicles illegally parked had a criminal record contrasted with 2 per cent of legally parked vehicles.

Aims of the research

This report examines the extent to which anti-social behaviour on the road is linked to criminal activity by analysing the criminal histories, current offending patterns and reconvictions of serious traffic offenders. The study also aims to answer questions about whether those who commit serious traffic offences are normally law-abiding members of the public or whether they are also likely to be involved with other types of criminal offending. As a second stage to the study, an examination of the policing of traffic incidents probes, in more depth, the connections between serious traffic offending and crime.

Format of the report

The remainder of the report is structured as follows:

- Section 2 provides details of the methodology involved in carrying out this study.
- Section 3 examines the socio-demographic profile of serious traffic offenders using findings from the Home Office Offenders Index (OI) and the Young People and Crime survey (YPAC).
- Section 4 details the offending patterns of serious traffic offenders; focusing on current and past offending, and also the risk of reconviction.
- Section 5 analyses interviews with traffic officers carried out in three police forces to highlight the types of offences that are discovered when policing traffic incidents and considers the process by which police deal with incidents.
- Finally, section 6 sets out conclusions and recommendations drawn from this work.

2.   **Methodology**

This study follows a two-stage design. The first stage examines the socio-demographic characteristics and the criminal histories of serious traffic offenders, and makes comparisons with other criminal offenders. Two existing data sources are used: the Home Office Offenders Index (OI), and a national survey, Young People and Crime (YPAC). For the second stage, interviews were carried out in a sample of three police forces, in order to investigate the policing of traffic incidents in relation to serious traffic offending.

Offenders Index

The OI holds the criminal histories of all those convicted of a 'standard list' offence in England and Wales from 1963 onwards.[6] In 1996 three serious traffic offences – driving in excess of the alcohol limit, driving whilst disqualified and dangerous driving – were added to the standard list, so records of convictions for these offences within the OI data start from 1 January 1996.

The sample used here consists of over 42,861 offenders. It comprises two cohorts of offenders convicted in:

(i)   the first fifteen days of March 1996; and

(ii)   the first fifteen days of November 1996.

The OI sample is large, with national coverage and comprehensive records of criminal convictions. It is the 1996 version of the 'official' sample used for the analysis of criminal histories in Criminal Statistics.[7] In this study, the focus is on comparisons between those convicted of serious traffic offences and other groups of offenders. A series of key measures were extracted from the data for all sample cases:

---

6   Standard list offences include all indictable or 'triable each way' offences and a few of the more serious summary offences.

7   See, for example, Home Office, 1998a: Chapter 9. It is clear from Criminal Statistics that, after appropriate comparisons with all offenders convicted in the given year, the sample is regarded as representative of the year's convictions. The sample analysed here is slightly larger (by some 3%) than that shown in Chapter 9 of Criminal Statistics, 1998, as we have not excluded convictions for breaches of previous sentences.

- For '**current**'[8] **court appearance**: number and types of offence, sex and age of offender.

- For **previous offending**: number of court appearances, number and types of offences, age at first conviction, time since previous court appearance.

Patterns of **recent offending** (for a ten month period) prior to current court appearance and **subsequent offending** (for a twelve-month period) following the court appearance are also examined using similar measures based on court appearances and numbers and types of offence conviction. These analyses cover a relatively short time-span before and after the 'current' court appearance, for periods when convictions for serious traffic offences were included in offenders' OI records.[9]

As a basis for the analysis, seven main groups of **offence** were identified:

- **Mainstream criminal offences**: violence, burglary, robbery, theft and handling, criminal damage, drug offences.

- **Car theft**: theft or unauthorised taking of a vehicle; theft from a vehicle.

- **Serious traffic offences**: drink driving, driving whilst disqualified, dangerous driving (including causing death).

- **Other standard list offences**: offences not classified within the specified main types of offence, or where the offence classification was not recorded.

- **Breaking bail and breach cases**: failing to surrender to bail; cases arising from a breach of the requirements or conditions of a previous sentence.

- **Summary motoring offences**: motoring offences that are not on the standard list.

- **Other summary offences**:[10] other offences (not including motoring offences) that are not standard list offences.

---

8   i.e. their conviction in either March or November 1996.
9   For recent offending patterns, the November 1996 section of the sample is utilised, and for the work on subsequent offending, the March 1996 section is used.
10 Convictions for summary motoring offences and other summary offences appear in the Offenders Index only when they are dealt with at a court appearance together with a standard list offence. They are considered only for specific sections of the data analysis.

The rationale for this grouping is explained more fully in Appendix A, where further details of the handling of the OI data are also given. The classification of offence types follows precedents used in *Criminal Statistics*; however, the groupings for serious traffic offences and for car theft have been devised for this study.[11] Serious traffic offences are often disaggregated into the three component categories.

An offender's court appearance often involves several charges, and multiple convictions may therefore result. The OI defines the *principal offence* by the most serious sentence given (Home Office, 1998a), and this study therefore regards the principal offence as the most important for classifying offenders. Table 2.1 shows the six *offender groups* defined by principal offence for this study. Three types of serious traffic offenders are distinguished: 'drink drivers' 'disqualified drivers' and 'dangerous drivers'. 'Car thieves' are an important group for comparisons, as are 'mainstream offenders' (the most numerous group); 'other offenders' covers those convicted of all remaining types of principal offence.

Table 2.1: *Offender groups: based on principal offence conviction at the sample court appearance.*

Offender group	Principal offence: the offences or offence groups included.	Number of offenders in sample	
		March 1996	November 1996
Drink drivers	drink driving (in excess of the alcohol limit)	2,451	2,717
Disqualified drivers	driving whilst disqualified	751	857
Dangerous drivers	dangerous driving (including causing death)	215	181
Car thieves	Theft or unauthorised taking of a vehicle (including aggravated taking and theft from a vehicle)	934	881
Mainstream offenders	Mainstream criminal offences: violence, burglary, robbery, theft and handling (non-vehicle), criminal damage, drug offences	11,548	11,478
Other offenders	all other offences	5,681	5,167
Totals		21,580	21,281

11 The 'mainstream' group excludes offences for which the research literature showed some prior evidence of specialisation in criminal careers; mainstream offenders thus become our key group for comparisons. Following Light et al (1993) the term 'car theft' is used to designate a group of offences that includes theft of and from a vehicle.

Young people and crime survey

YPAC is a major study investigating self-reports of offending, based primarily on "... a national random sample of 1,721 young people aged 14 to 25 (plus a booster sample of 808 young people from ethnic minorities) ... interviewed about their background, their family life, their school experiences and aspects of their current lifestyle" (Graham and Bowling, 1995: ix).[12] Respondents were asked about their involvement in 33 different criminal offences (see Appendix B). Five serious traffic offences were included, namely:

- **Licence and insurance offences**: 'driven a car, motorcycle or moped on a public road without licence and/or insurance'.

- **Drink driving**: 'driven a car, motorcycle or moped knowing you had drunk more than the legal limit'.

- **Dangerous driving**: 'driven a car, motorcycle or moped in a dangerous or reckless manner'.

- **Disqualified driving**: 'driven a car, motorcycle or moped when you were disqualified from driving by a court'.

- **Accident offences**: 'had an accident when driving a car, motorcycle or moped, without stopping to see what happened or reporting it to the police'.

Although these descriptions, embedded as they are in survey questions, do not constitute exact legal definitions, it is clear that they correspond to distinct offence types. Respondents were asked whether they had committed offences 'ever' and 'in the last year'.[13]

Analysis of the YPAC survey was carried out to support the findings from the OI data and to provide further information regarding the sociodemographic profile of serious traffic offenders. This secondary analysis of the survey data followed as far as possible the precedents of Graham and Bowling's report; for example in relying on weighted estimates of percentages and other statistics[14] and in basing most tabulations on the 'core sample' (except for the analysis of ethnicity).

---

12 Graham and Bowling checked their sample against several other sources and found it to be broadly representative of the general population, although younger respondents, students, the unemployed and those on youth training schemes were somewhat over-represented, and older respondents and those from poorer localities were slightly under-represented (1995:107). The ethnic minority booster sample was also found to be skewed towards those who lived in areas with high concentrations of ethnic minorities.

13 The number of young people reporting disqualified driving and accident offences were too low for separate analysis, but these data are included in measures based on all serious traffic offending.

14 In Graham and Bowling's analyses, re-weighting was used, to correct for unequal selection probabilities, which '[made] the national sample representative of young people in the population.' (1995:108). This system of weighting was also used throughout the analysis for the current report.

Age-groups

The age groups used in this report are: 10–15, 16–17, 18–20, 21–25, 26–32, and 33 or more. In setting up this age grouping four factors were relevant:

(i) the findings from criminal careers research on peak ages of onset of offending (and desistance);

(ii) the legal distinctions between juveniles, young offenders and adults within the criminal justice system;

(iii) the age-categories used in *Criminal Statistics*; and

(iv) the minimum legal ages for driving and motor cycling.

In some analyses the first three groups are combined (as 10–20) but in others they are kept separate. For the YPAC survey data, (where the maximum age of respondents was 25), the main age groups were 16–17, 18–20 and 21–25.[15]

Interviews in a sample of forces

Interviews with 132 traffic police officers in three forces (designated A, B and C) were undertaken during six weeks of intensive field-work (two weeks with each force). This followed three days preliminary work with Force A, to enable piloting of interview questions. Appendix C shows the questions used for the interviews. Access to officers varied according to their work schedules, and agreements reached with the forces' senior officers. Two forces preferred 'office-based' interviewing, making officers available at specific times. In the third force, most of the interviews were conducted in patrol cars during 'down-time' whilst officers were on routine patrol. Throughout the fieldwork, efforts were made to ensure that in each force the sample of officers was as representative as possible of the spread of operational experience within each unit or divisional group. Nearly 50 per cent of the total of officers working at that time at the research sites were interviewed.[16]

---

15 The survey showed that personal access to motor vehicles increases rapidly between the ages of 16 and 25.

16 The number interviewed was not less than 40% for any one division or unit. To some extent, sampling was constrained by shift and roster systems that determined officers' availability for interview at any given time. A summary of the sample numbers is given in Appendix C (Table C1); in two forces a small number of managers, and those with more specialist roles (such as the local intelligence officer) were included.

The sample is limited in two main respects. First, in the choice of the three forces, it was a requirement that each had an organisational structure that (at minimum) involved clearly identifiable groups of traffic officers. Second, within the two forces with devolved structures for road policing, the sample of divisional officers was restricted to specific divisions.[17] Of course, a sample of three forces cannot be argued to be nationally representative in any strict statistical sense, however carefully they are selected. In essence, Stage 2 of the study is an exploratory case study, and the limitations of the data must be taken into account when interpreting the findings.

The interviews themselves were undertaken using CAPI (computer-assisted personal interview) methods. The questionnaire – which took 30 to 40 minutes – was set up on a notebook computer enabling answers to be entered directly in a coded form or (for some questions) verbatim. All interviews were carried out by the same researcher.

---

17 Under Force C's devolved management structure, each division had different organisational arrangements to provide for traffic policing, and in some divisions it would have been difficult to identify officers specialising in traffic. We were therefore guided in the choice of a division by this factor.

3. Socio-demographic profile of serious traffic offenders

This section gives details of the gender, age and social background of serious traffic offenders and provides an important backdrop to the profile of offending histories given in the next section. Assessments of offenders based on age and gender are possible using the OI sample, although this data is limited as it does not provide any details of the social backgrounds of offenders. However, socio-demographic factors can be gleaned from the YPAC survey, which is used to provide further information on ethnicity and socio-economic status.

Gender of serious traffic offenders

Figure 3.1 shows the gender distribution of all offenders in the OI sample. Serious traffic offending was found to be chiefly a male activity, and females were involved far less than they were in other kinds of offending. The percentages of females were:

- 13 per cent for 'mainstream' crime;
- 8 per cent for drink driving;
- below 3 per cent for disqualified driving;
- below 5 per cent for dangerous driving; and
- 3.4 per cent for car theft.

The disproportionate involvement of males in serious traffic offending and vehicle-related crime reflected well established findings, for example in the annual statistics on *Motoring Offences* (see Home Office, 1998b).

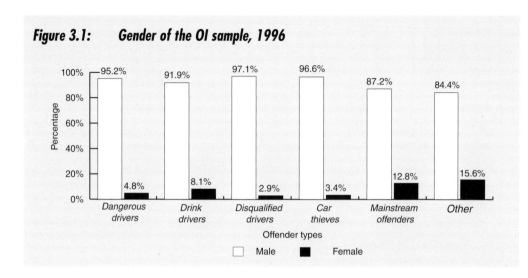

Figure 3.1:   Gender of the OI sample, 1996

The YPAC survey further supported these findings. Figures 3.2 and 3.3 show the prevalence of the three more commonly reported serious traffic offences by gender of the respondents.[18] Figure 3.2 shows the percentage of males and females that reported that they had 'ever' committed each of these offences and Figure 3.3 shows those respondents who reported committing such offences in the last year. As found in the OI sample, serious traffic offences were found to be more prevalent amongst males than females although the differences are less extreme.

Figure 3.2:   YPAC survey: percentage of young people aged 16 to 25 who admitted 'ever' committing serious traffic offences, by gender

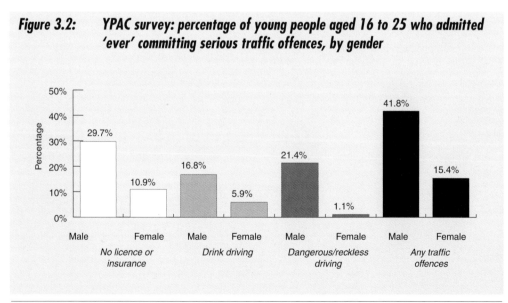

18 As noted in section 2, the number of young people admitting disqualified driving and accident offences were too low for separate analysis, but where these offences were reported, they are included in measures of all serious traffic offending.

The survey showed that 42 per cent of males had 'ever' committed a serious traffic offence, nearly three times the level of 15 per cent for females. Twenty-two per cent of males had committed a traffic offence in the last year, again nearly three times the rate of 8 per cent for females. Licence and insurance offences were the most common for both sexes; this may have been indicative of the younger age of the respondents. Females were much less likely to commit dangerous or reckless driving offences than males, however the differences between males and females in the tendency to drink and drive were less pronounced.

Figure 3.3: **YPAC survey: percentage of young people aged 16 to 25 who admitted committing serious traffic offences 'in the last year', by gender**

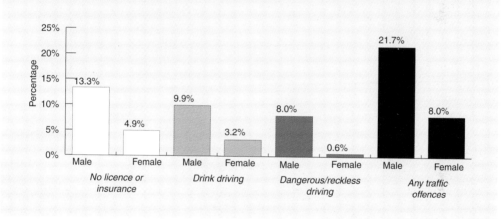

Summary - gender

Offenders Index

- Serious traffic offending was found to be chiefly a *male* activity, and females were involved far less than they were in other kinds of offending.
- Convicted *females* made up 13% of mainstream offenders, however 8% of drink drivers, less than 3% of disqualified drivers and less than 5% of dangerous drivers were female.

Young people and crime survey

- 42% of young *male* respondents had 'ever' committed a traffic offence and 22% had committed a traffic offence 'in the last year'.
- Only 15% of young *female* respondents had 'ever' committed a traffic offence and 8% had committed such an offence 'in the last year'.

- Driving without a licence or insurance was the most frequent traffic offence both for young males and young females.

Age of serious traffic offenders

The OI data showed that drink drivers tend to be significantly older than other groups of offenders, with some 48 per cent aged 33 or more, in contrast to figures within this age-group of 26 per cent for disqualified drivers, 22 per cent for dangerous drivers and 21 per cent for mainstream offenders (see Table 3.1). The age profiles of disqualified drivers and dangerous drivers were broadly similar to that of mainstream offenders; for each of these groups between 60 per cent and 75 per cent of offenders were in the age-range 18 to 32.[19] In contrast, the profile for car thieves was very distinctive, with nearly 20 per cent below age 16, and over 40 per cent aged 16 to 20 (more than twice the percentage for mainstream offenders in these age-groups). Further calculations from the OI data showed that the highest age-specific conviction rates for drink driving and disqualified driving were between 21 and 25, whereas for dangerous driving and for mainstream crime the peak age of offending was between 18 and 20.

---

19 Serious traffic offenders are unlikely to be below the minimum legal age for driving or motor cycling, so the percentage of cases below age 16 is very small.

Table 3.1:   Age distribution of the OI sample, 1996

Age (years)	Dangerous drivers	Drink drivers	Disqualified drivers	Car thieves	Mainstream offenders	Other offenders
10 to 15	2.8%	0.2%	0.9%	19.1%	10.2%	3.7%
16 and 17	3.8%	0.7%	1.2%	13.3%	5.2%	3.3%
18 to 20	20.2%	7.2%	12.3%	31.2%	16.9%	15.7%
21 to 25	30.1%	19.4%	30.7%	22.6%	23.7%	27.3%
26 to 32	21.7%	24.5%	28.5%	9.0%	23.0%	23.7%
33 or more	21.5%	47.9%	26.4%	4.7%	20.9%	26.2%

The YPAC survey provides an additional perspective on serious traffic offending among the younger age-groups (Table 3.2). Nearly half of all male respondents between 21 and 25 years reported having 'ever' committed a traffic offence. This could be broken down as follows: 31 per cent of males admitted to a licence/insurance offence, 24 per cent to drink driving and 25 per cent to dangerous driving. The figures for females aged 21 to 25 were below the rates for males, with 17 per cent reporting any traffic offence, (12% admitting licence/insurance offences, 7.5% drink driving, and only 1% dangerous driving). For both males and females, the rates for 18 to 20 year-olds were generally lower than the figures for the older age group, and those for the 16 to 17 age-group were smaller again.

The prevalence of offending can best be measured from 'current participation', that is, reported rates of offending in the last year. Serious traffic offending seemed to peak between the ages of 18 and 20, when nearly 30 per cent of males and 12 per cent of females reported current participation. This finding also echoed Farrington's comments that "... the peak desistance rate is at age 21-25" for mainstream criminal offending[20] (1994: 566).

---

20 Although Farrington does not distinguish between males and females in this statement, his evidence is based largely on studies of males. Based on self-report data, Graham and Bowling (1995: x-xi) suggested that the peak age of onset for mainstream offending by females is similar to that for males, but that desistance among females may peak at an earlier age than for males.

Table 3.2: ***YPAC survey: prevalence of young people admitting serious traffic offences, by age and gender***

		Age (years)		
	Gender	16 and 17	18 to 20	21 to 25
Cumulative participation: Have you *ever* done this?				
No licence or insurance	Male	21.5%	35.1%	30.7%
	Female	9.2%	11.4%	11.6%
Drink driving	Male	6.0%	16.1%	23.9%
	Female	0.8%	7.5%	7.5%
Dangerous/reckless driving	Male	12.6%	23.1%	25.4%
	Female	1.2%	0.7%	1.3%
Committed any traffic offences	Male	26.9%	43.2%	49.4%
	Female	9.2%	17.8%	17.1%
Current participation: Have you done this *in the last year?*				
No licence or insurance	Male	11.4%	15.2%	13.0%
	Female	6.5%	6.3%	2.7%
Drink driving	Male	4.9%	14.3%	9.5%
	Female	0.8%	6.0%	2.2%
Dangerous/reckless driving	Male	6.3%	13.8%	4.7%
	Female	1.2%	0.2%	0.6%
Committed any traffic offences	Male	17.4%	29.8%	18.2%
	Female	7.3%	11.6%	5.5%

Summary - age

Offenders Index

- 48% of drink drivers were 33 years or older.

- Disqualified drivers and dangerous drivers had a similar age profile to mainstream offenders – between 60% and 75% were aged between 18 and 32 years.

- The highest conviction rates for drink driving and disqualified driving were in the age group 21 to 25. Rates of dangerous driving and mainstream crime peaked earlier between 18 to 20 years.

Young people and crime survey

- By age 21 to 25 nearly 50% of males admitted committing a serious traffic offence in comparison to 17% of females. The most common offence was driving without a licence or insurance.

- Thirty percent of males and 12% of females admitted a serious traffic offence in the last year. Serious traffic offending peaked in the 18 to 20 age group.

Social factors and serious traffic offending

Access to a vehicle

The prevalence rates for serious traffic offending in the YPAC survey are also dependent on whether the respondent has access to a vehicle. The survey data included questions on this topic and found that males show higher rates of access to vehicles within each age-group; by age 21 to 25, 70 per cent of males reported that they had a vehicle available to them, with the corresponding figure for females being 61 per cent. For the youngest age-group (16-17 years), the percentages were naturally much lower; the majority - 86 per cent of females and 73 per cent of males - had no vehicle available to them. The importance of this distinction is confirmed when looking at the break down of rates of prevalence for overall serious traffic offending for the last year. While 32 per cent of males with access to a vehicle committed a serious traffic offence, only 8 per cent of those without access committed such an offence. The corresponding rates of serious traffic offending for females were 12 per cent (with access) and 4 per cent (without access).

Ethnicity and the serious traffic offender

Analysis of ethnicity has followed the same approach as that of Graham and Bowling (1995), using data from all samples (including the booster sample). Figure 3.4 contrasts white respondents with five other main ethnic categories. The prevalence of 'ever' traffic offending was significantly lower within each of the ethnic groups in comparison with the white sample, for both males and females. For example, the percentage for white males (44%) was higher than the rates for the Indian and Pakistani groups (27% and 29%) with other ethnic groups showing even lower rates.

For females who have 'ever' offended, the 16 per cent figure for the white group was considerably greater than the rates for all other ethnic groups, and most of the Asian female groups (Bangladeshi, Indian, Pakistani, and other Asian) showed very low rates of prevalence. A similar picture was evident from the figures on serious traffic offending 'last year', with significantly lower figures for the minority ethnic groups, both for males and females. The sharpest contrast was between Asian and white females.

It could be argued that these differences may be due to a reluctance to admit serious traffic offences amongst ethnic groups. This does not appear to be the case, as Graham and Bowling did not suggest any reservations when interpreting similar data for mainstream offending and for drug use (1995: Table 3.3). Indeed the survey questions on serious traffic offending are arguably less intrusive than questions on more serious criminal offending and on the use of drugs; if there was a differential reluctance to report offending, Graham and Bowling would have recognised it in earlier analyses.

The question of whether the ethnic groups' lesser involvement in serious traffic offending could be explained by a lower level of access to vehicles is tested in Table 3.3. This shows that within both the 'access' and 'no access' groups there were considerable differences between the prevalence rates for offending in the last year. For example, of those with access to a vehicle, 32 per cent of white males reported offending, compared with 20 per cent of black and Asian males. The differences between the white group and the black and Asian group was even sharper where respondents had no personal access to a vehicle (9.7% and 3.7% respectively). Ethnic differences for females showed a similar picture to that of males. Overall, Table 3.3 confirms the finding of higher rates of serious traffic offending among young white people compared to other ethnic groups.

Figure 3.4: Serious traffic offending, by ethnic group and gender: young people age 16-25

Traffic offences 'ever'

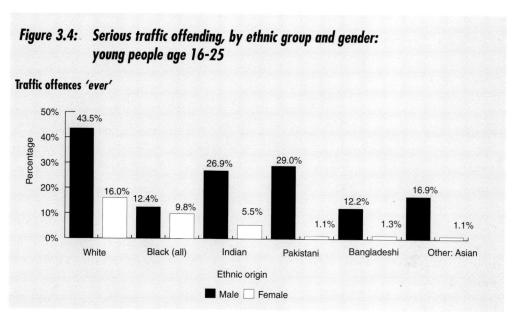

Traffic offences in the 'last year'

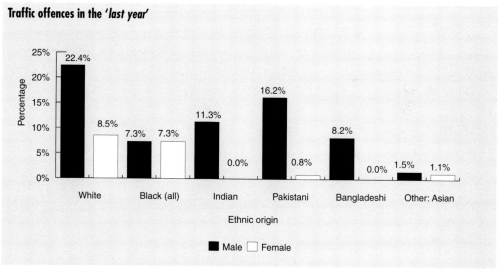

Note: The sample size (N) for these graphs are as follows: Males: White N=532; Black (all) N=72; Indian N=91; Pakistani N=93; Bangladeshi N=36; Other Asian N=36. Females: White N=685; Black (all) N=97; Indian N=76; Pakistani N=66; Bangladeshi N=44; Other Asian N=35.

Table 3.3: *Serious traffic offending committed in the 'last year', by ethnic group, gender and vehicle access: young people aged 16-25*

	Male		Female	
	White	Black and Asian	White	Black and Asian
No vehicle access Any traffic offences in the last year?	9.7% (n=246)	3.7% (n=201)	5.2% (n=403)	0.7% (n=231)
Vehicle access Any traffic offences in the last year?	31.6% (n=286)	20.4% (n=127)	11.6% (n=282)	6.5% (n=87)
All cases	22.4% (n=532)	10.3% (n=328)	8.5% (n=685)	2.2% (n=318)

Summary - ethnicity

- Forty four percent of young white males admitted ever committing a serious traffic offence in comparison to 29% of young Pakistani males and less for other ethnic groups.

- Sixteen percent of young white females admitted ever committing a serious traffic offence in contrast with 10% of young black females and less for the other ethnic groups.

- A similar profile was shown for offences over the last year with other ethnic groups committing fewer offences than young white people; this difference remained after taking account of access to a vehicle.

Socio-economic status and serious traffic offenders

The YPAC survey distinguishes between four socio-economic (SES) categories based mainly on family of origin.[21] For general offending the survey found that SES was related to offending for females, but for males the relationship was not statistically significant. Figure 3.5 shows the relationship between SES and overall serious traffic offending both for cumulative (ever) participation and for current (last year) participation.

---

21 Graham and Bowling (1995:33) noted that this measure of SES was based on a standard classification of occupational groups, using father's occupation or (if this were not available) mother's occupation or respondent's own occupation if they were in employment. 'A' denotes the highest social class and 'E' the lowest.

The figures for cumulative participation for males were not significantly different between the four SES groups. However, for male offending in the last year there were differences, with the 30 per cent rate for SES group A/B considerably in excess of the figures for the other three groups. When male offending in the last year was disaggregated into the three main offence groups (see Appendix B, Table B2) there was a significant difference only for drink driving. The 20 per cent drink driving rate for SES group A/B was over twice the level for any of the other SES categories.[22] For young males the only significant effect of SES on current serious traffic offending may therefore be that those in the highest social class group are more likely to drink and drive.

Further analysis showed that the even pattern between the SES groups in the 'ever' rates for male serious traffic offending concealed two counterbalancing trends. The rate for drink driving was highest for the A/B group, but the rate for no licence/insurance tended to be higher for the C2 and DE groups (see Appendix B, Table B2). Confidence can be given to the finding of higher rates for drink driving amongst the A/B socio-economic group, since it is evident in both the 'last year' and 'ever' analyses. Although there was certainly a suggestion of more licence/insurance offences among the C2 and DE socio-economic groups there was less confidence in this finding, since it was not replicated in the data on offending in the last year.

---

22 If comparisons between SES groups are confined to males with access to a vehicle, the contrast is even sharper; just over 30% of the A/B group admit drink driving in the last year, compared with less than 10% in each of the other three SES groups.

Figure 3.5: Socio-economic status and serious traffic offending: young people aged 16-25

Traffic offences 'ever'

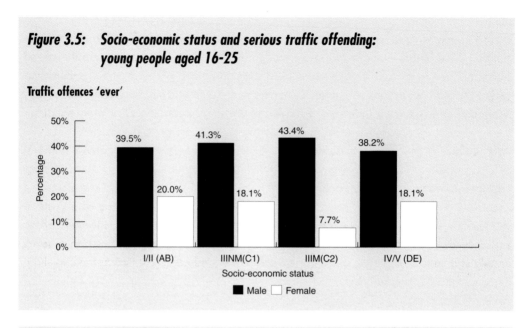

Traffic offences in the 'last year'

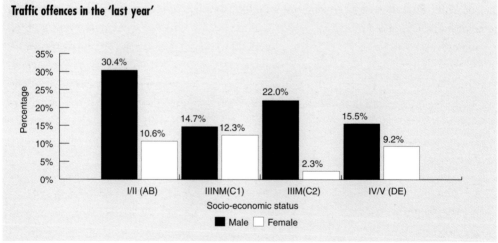

For females, Figure 3.5 shows statistically significant differences for both last year's offending and cumulative participation for SES and female offenders, yet in both cases this was due entirely to an extremely low rate for the C2 socio-economic group. More detailed analysis showed it would be difficult to draw any safe conclusions about the relationship of SES to serious traffic offending for females.[23]

---

23 Further investigation for the separate offences of no licence/insurance and for drink driving (and also for age and access to a vehicle) generally confirmed the low level of offending for females in the C2 group, but also showed other low rates of offending within specific SES groups. As far as we know, there are no suggestions in the literature about why an intermediate social class group (either male or female) should be especially law-abiding.

Overall, there were perhaps less clear relationships between SES and serious traffic offending than might have been anticipated, although we must also be mindful of the debate about the results of self-report studies in relation to social class. As Graham and Bowling pointed out in their review of previous research (1995: 34) many self-report studies have found no association (or only a weak association) between social class and offending.

'Adverse factors' and serious traffic offending

The YPAC survey considers a number of factors associated with the family, experience of school and delinquent peers. A simple 'adverse factor score' was calculated on a scale of zero to four; scores were constructed separately for males and females, since some of the predictors of offending differed between the sexes. Adverse factor scores were shown to be strongly related to mainstream offending for both males and females (Graham and Bowling, 1995: 47-48).

It was found that, for males this same adverse factor score was also strongly related to serious traffic offending; the percentage of males reporting serious traffic offences (based on cumulative participation) rises from 16 per cent for score zero to 79 per cent for score four. For females, there was also a significant (but slightly weaker) association between adverse factor score and serious traffic offending; the percentage reporting serious traffic offences rises from 10 per cent (scores zero and 1) to 27 per cent at score four. Further details and results of the analysis are given in Appendix B. Overall, these are very clear indications that serious traffic offending is related to family, school and peer group factors.

Summary - SES

- In general, there was not a strong relationship between socio-economic group and overall rates of serious traffic offending, for either males or females.

- Males in the highest social groups were more than twice as likely to admit drink driving offences in the 'last year' as any other social group; a similar pattern, with the highest rates among the A/B groups, was evident from the figures on 'ever' drink driving among males.

- Males in the lowest social groups were more likely to admit 'ever' committing a licence and insurance offence, although this finding was not replicated for offending in the 'last year'.

- Social factors such as family, peer group and school that have been found to correlate strongly with mainstream offending were also found to be related to serious traffic offending.

Summary

Gender - OI

- Serious traffic offending was found to be predominantly a *male* activity. Among convicted offenders, females made up only 8% of drink drivers, less than 3% of disqualified drivers and less than 5% of dangerous drivers. Among mainstream offenders, 13% were female.

Age - OI

- 48% of convicted drink drivers were found to be 33 years or older.

- The age-profiles of disqualified drivers and dangerous drivers were broadly similar to that of mainstream offenders, with between 60% and 75% of offenders between ages 18 and 32.

- The highest conviction rates for drink driving and disqualified driving were in the age-group 21-25, whereas for mainstream offending and dangerous driving the peak age-group was 18-20 year olds.

Young people aged 16 to 25

- The YPAC survey showed that among 21-25 year olds, nearly 50% of males and 17% of females report 'ever' committing a serious traffic offence.

- The peak age for serious traffic offending was 18-20. In this age-group, 30% of males and 12% of females reported committing a serious traffic offence in the 'last year'.

Ethnicity

- Among young people, prevalence of serious traffic offending was found to be significantly higher for both males and females in the white sample compared to other ethnic groups.

Social factors

- The YPAC survey showed that males in the higher social class groups were more likely to drink and drive, and suggested that the lower social class groups may be more likely to commit licence and insurance offences.

4.

Offending patterns of
serious traffic offenders

In this section the offending patterns of serious traffic offenders are studied through their criminal histories. The analysis focuses on linkages between 'mainstream' criminal offending, vehicle theft and the three serious traffic offences included (from 1996) in the Offenders Index. These offences are:

- drink driving;
- disqualified driving; and
- dangerous driving.

The analysis will examine 'current' court convictions, past offending behaviour and reconvictions. Findings from the YPAC survey will be used in support of the discussion of offending patterns.

Current convictions

At their 1996 'sample' court appearance[24], the 42,681 offenders in the OI sample were convicted of a total of 97,997 offences, an average of 2.29 offences per appearance. Forty percent of offenders were convicted of more than one offence, with the remaining 60 per cent each being found guilty of a single offence.

Figures 4.1 and 4.2 show how the average number of offences varies between offender groups.[25] Disqualified drivers, dangerous drivers and car thieves were each convicted of three or more offences at this appearance. However, it is routine police procedure to investigate whether charges should be brought for summary motoring offences (arising from untaxed vehicles, driving licence irregularities or 'construction and use' offences, and so on) when individuals are charged with serious traffic offences and car theft. About a third of the secondary offence convictions for serious traffic offenders were accounted for by summary motoring offences. If summary motoring offences were omitted, the mean number of convictions was remarkably similar at around 2.0 in all offender categories except car thieves (higher, at 2.45) and drink drivers (much lower at 1.17). Drink drivers were the most likely to be charged with a single offence, and multiple convictions occurred in only 12 per cent of such cases. All other offender groups showed at least 40 per cent of cases with more than one conviction.

---

24 Either during the first 15 days of March 1996, or the first 15 days of November 1996 (See Section 2 for details).
25 See Section 2 for the definition of offender groups.

Figure 4.1: *OI sample, 1996: the number of convictions at current court appearance, by offender group*

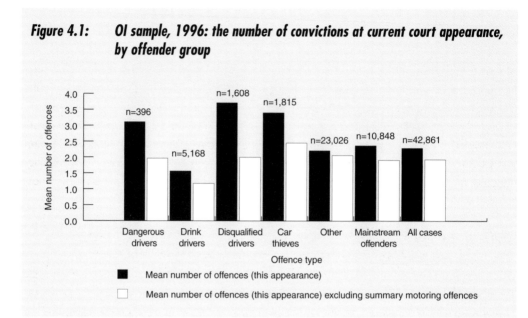

Figure 4.2: *OI sample, 1996: the percentage of offenders convicted of more than one offence at current court appearance, by offender group*

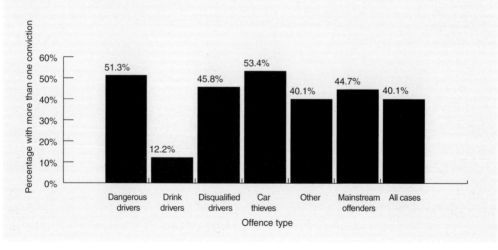

Types of multiple convictions

Types of multiple convictions were found to vary considerably, but with systematic differences between offender groups. An examination of 'secondary' offences[26] (see Table 4.1) showed that some 15 per cent of disqualified drivers and dangerous drivers were also convicted of a mainstream offence (compared with 22% of car thieves). Only small percentages of serious traffic offenders had additional convictions for car theft, but 18 per cent of car thieves had secondary convictions for serious traffic offences. This finding reflected the relative seriousness of the two types of offence: where an offender was charged with both, car theft was generally regarded as the principal offence.

Table 4.1: **OI sample, 1996: the percentage of offenders convicted of each type of secondary offence at the current court appearance**

Secondary offences	Offender groups					
	Dangerous drivers	Drink drivers	Disqualified drivers	Car thieves	Other offenders	Mainstream offenders
Mainstream offences	14.9%	2.3%	14.4%	21.8%	16.4%	
Other standard list offences	8.6%	1.5%	7.9%	6.3%	43.9%	5.3%
Bail breaks or breaches	7.6%	3.9%	13.3%	15.2%	39.7%	12.1%
Vehicle theft offences	4.5%	0.9%	5.7%		2.4%	3.4%
Serious traffic offences				18.3%	3.1%	2.0%
Summary motor offences	49.5%	21.8%	97.4%	40.3%	15.0%	4.3%
Other summary offences	2.8%	1.0%	3.7%	3.7%	19.7%	5.3%
Valid n	*396*	*5,168*	*1,608*	*1,815*	*10,848*	*23,026*

Naturally, serious traffic offences may also occur as 'secondary convictions'. Overall, there was a total of 9,597 serious traffic convictions in the OI sample; some 15 per cent of these stemmed from court appearances where the principal offence was a mainstream offence, other offence or a car theft. About a third of the 3,439 offences of disqualified driving were accounted for in this way, in contrast to drink driving offences, where the figure was only 6 per cent.

---

26 Convictions other than that for the principal offence, at the sample court appearance.

Some court appearances may involve two or more convictions for serious traffic offending (often as a result of one 'traffic incident'):

- Where dangerous driving was the principal offence, only one such charge was brought in about two-thirds of cases, however, in 18 per cent of cases there was a drink driving conviction, and 15 per cent of cases involved disqualified driving.

- In 4 per cent of drink driving cases, disqualified driving was also involved.

- Where the principal offence was disqualified driving, 19 per cent of cases had two or more such charges. In about 7 per cent of cases, there were secondary convictions for drink driving.

Summary – current convictions

- 40% of the sample were convicted of more than one offence at their current court appearance.

- The three types of serious traffic offence showed different patterns in the extent to which they were (or were not) intertwined with other kinds of offending, although dangerous driving and disqualified driving showed some broad similarities.

- Only 12% of drink drivers were convicted of secondary offences; for disqualified drivers and dangerous drivers, the percentage was over 45%.

- Serious traffic offenders were commonly charged with summary motoring offences, which accounted for a third of their secondary offence convictions.

- 15% of dangerous drivers and disqualified drivers were also convicted of a mainstream offence.

- 18% of car thieves were also convicted of a serious traffic offence.

Past offending behaviour

Past offending behaviour patterns are examined in two ways:

(i)   analysis of all cases in the OI sample; and

(ii)   analysis of past offending of the OI sample convicted in November 1996 over the previous ten month period.[27]

---

27 Although only a short time period, this sample includes previous convictions for the three serious traffic offences incorporated in the OI since January 1996.

Previous offending of the whole OI sample

There are four OI offence groups for which complete previous convictions are recorded: mainstream offences; other standard list offences; breaking bail and breach cases and car theft. Measures of 'total' criminal history (over the lifetime of an offender) must be based on convictions for these four offence groups. The remaining three offence groups are omitted because of incomplete records.[28]

Figure 4.3: OI sample, 1996: the percentage of offenders with previous convictions, by offender group

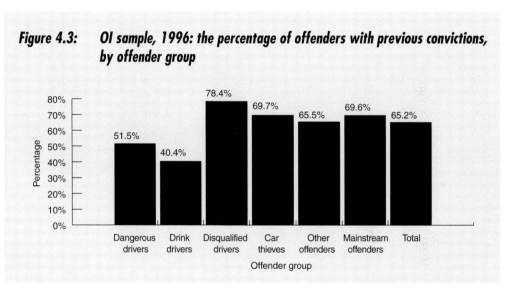

Sixty-five percent of the 42,861 offenders in the 1996 sample had previous convictions; Figure 4.3 shows how the percentage varied between offender groups. The most extreme values were for two groups of serious traffic offenders, with drink drivers the lowest at 40 per cent, and disqualified drivers the highest at 78 per cent. Dangerous drivers showed the second lowest figure at 51 per cent.

Prevalence of previous convictions

Table 4.2 shows the *prevalence*[29] of previous convictions for each type of offence; for every offender group the most common involvement was in mainstream crime. Indeed, the

---

28 The three offence groups omitted are: serious traffic offences themselves (since convictions were not recorded on the OI prior to 1996); summary motoring offences (since previous convictions will only appear in offenders' records if they are dealt with at the same court appearance as a standard list conviction); and (for the same reasons) other summary non-standard list offences.

29 Prevalence refers to the rate (or percentage) of offenders committing an offence of a given type (whatever the *number* of such offences).

offender groups showed broad similarities in their types of previous offending (allowing for the generally lower level of involvement of the drink drivers group and the higher involvement of disqualified drivers). Overall, the data on prevalence in Table 4.2 shows little indication of specialisation (although the figures necessarily exclude previous traffic offending). The figures for previous mainstream offending show similar patterns to those for total offending with disqualified drivers again the highest at 73 per cent. For previous car theft, the figure for disqualified drivers was slightly higher (at 51%) than for car thieves (at 48%) although this might be accounted for by the different age-profiles of the two groups. The low level of previous car theft amongst drink drivers (15%) is especially notable; it is much lower than the 31 per cent for mainstream offenders.

Table 4.2:   *Prevalence of previous convictions for five types of offence, by offender group*

	Offender groups						
Previous convictions: type of offence	Dangerous drivers	Drink drivers	Disqualified drivers	Car thieves	Other offenders	Mainstream offenders	**All cases**
Mainstream offences	46.7%	36.4%	72.8%	63.1%	59.9%	66.7%	**61.2%**
Other standard list offences	22.7%	13.2%	42.4%	27.2%	31.1%	30.3%	**28.7%**
Bail breaks or breaches	26.5%	10.6%	52.1%	39.2%	36.6%	37.5%	**34.6%**
Vehicle theft offences	30.3%	15.1%	51.2%	48.4%	29.0%	31.0%	**30.1%**
Valid n	*396*	*5,168*	*1,608*	*1,815*	*10,848*	*23,026*	***42,861***

Incidence of previous convictions

Table 4.3 focuses on the 27,954 offenders who have previous convictions, and shows the *incidence*[30] of previous criminality through four basic indicators. There were many differences between offender groups. For drink drivers with a previous record, the average number of previous appearances (4.2) was significantly below the figures for other groups, and they showed about half as many convictions (7.2) as the sample as a whole (14.5). Only 28 per cent had a conviction before age 16, and the average time since the previous court appearance was over 8 years, substantially longer than other offender groups. To summarise, on each indicator drink drivers had a substantially lower level of previous

---

30 Incidence refers to measures of the level of criminality, for example the number of offences committed

criminality than mainstream offenders (or other groups). Compared to other groups, dangerous drivers showed slightly lower levels of previous criminality on each indicator, whereas disqualified drivers had marginally higher levels than mainstream offenders.

Table 4.3: **Offenders with previous convictions: incidence of previous criminality, by offender group**

| Incidence Indicators | Offender groups | | | | | | All cases |
	Dangerous drivers	Drink drivers	Disqualified drivers	Car thieves	Other offenders	Mainstream offenders	
Mean number of previous court appearances	6.1	4.2	8.2	5.9	6.8	7.2	**6.9**
Mean number of previous offences	13.2	7.2	17.7	14.9	14.0	15.3	**14.5**
% convicted before 16 years	41.7%	27.7%	41.6%	48.4%	33.6%	40.0%	**37.9%**
Mean number of months since last court appearance	44.4	101.3	28.3	15.4	33.5	30.8	**36.0**
Valid n	204	2,087	1,260	1,265	7,109	16,029	**27,954**

Age, gender and previous offending

Previous record is associated with age and sex. As Figure 4.4 shows, for each offender group the percentage of females with previous convictions was significantly below the figure for males; the sex difference was greater for dangerous drivers and drink drivers (and for car thieves) than for other offender groups. The number of female serious traffic offenders with previous convictions was in fact very small, with only 92 in the OI sample over the three offender groups.

Figure 4.4: The percentage of offenders with previous convictions, by offender group and gender

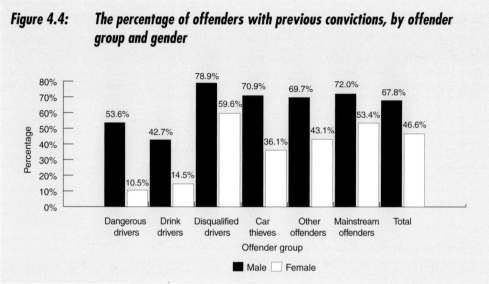

Table 4.4 shows the age of offenders for males only, as the number of female offenders is too small to break down by age group. Although the percentage of offenders with previous convictions increased between the three younger age groups, there was a slight decrease for those aged 33 or more (except for car thieves). For each age group, disqualified drivers showed a high percentage of previous convictions and drink drivers the lowest figure of all groups. The percentage of dangerous drivers with previous convictions was less than the comparable figure for mainstream offenders at each age. After taking account of age and sex, the differences between the criminal histories of offender groups were still evident.

Table 4.4: Percentage of male offenders with previous convictions: by age group

Age (years)	Offender groups						All cases
	Dangerous drivers	Drink drivers	Disqualified drivers	Car thieves	Other offenders	Mainstream offenders	
10 to 20	46.7%	23.2%	77.8%	63.6%	64.4%	57.1%	**58.4%**
	n=105	n=384	n= 225	n=1,110	n=2,186	n=6,586	n=10,596
21 to 25	50.0%	38.3%	82.7%	81.2%	70.2%	76.4%	**71.0%**
	n=116	n=929	n=485	n=404	n=2,520	n=4,772	n=9,226
26 to 32	64.6%	48.2%	80.6%	86.3%	75.3%	82.0%	**75.6%**
	n=79	n=1,164	n=438	n=160	n=2,102	n=4,606	n=8,549
33 or more	57.1%	44.9%	73.4%	88.8%	69.1%	79.6%	**68.1%**
	n=77	n=2,270	n=413	n=80	n=2,349	n=4,113	n=9,302

Case study: the criminality of drink drivers

Given the relatively low rate of previous offending among drink drivers it is interesting to compare this to the level of criminality within the general population. Comparisons can be made with the *Criminal Statistics* for birth cohorts (Home Office, 1998a).[31] The published data allow us to make comparisons for the 21 to 25 and the 26 to 32 age groups, for males and females. The results, shown in Figure 4.5, indicate that drink drivers were approximately twice as likely to have a criminal record as members of the general population of the same age and gender. For example, 38 per cent of male drink drivers aged 21 to 25 had a previous conviction, which compared with a figure of between 19 per cent and 20 per cent within the general population.[32] The criminality demonstrated here for drink drivers is modest (for example compared with disqualified drivers) but on this evidence there is certainly some relationship between having a criminal record and the likelihood of being convicted for drink driving.

Figure 4.5: **Percentage of drink drivers with previous convictions, compared to general population estimates**

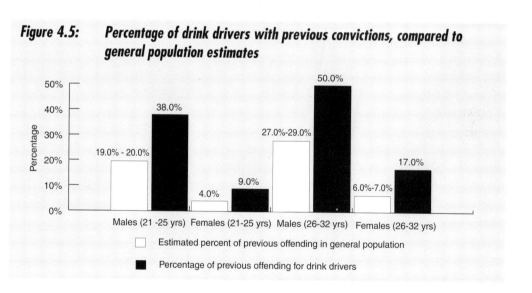

Estimated percent of previous offending in general population

Percentage of previous offending for drink drivers

---

31 Comparisons cannot be absolutely precise, for several reasons: the estimates differ quite substantially between cohorts, so there is no one figure for (for example) the proportion of 30 year old males who have a conviction; there are no estimates of early conviction rates for cohorts born later than 1973; and, estimates are made up to specific ages (currently, for example, age 23 for the 1973 cohort) and are updated periodically rather than annually.

32 These findings are also consistent with Riley's (1985) analysis based on self-report data for mainstream offending and drink driving.

Summary – previous convictions

- 65% of the whole OI sample had one or more previous convictions.

- 78% of disqualified drivers had a previous conviction, in comparison to 70% of mainstream offenders, 52% of dangerous drivers and 40% of drink drivers.

- For all offender groups the most common kind of previous conviction was mainstream offending; the profiles of each offender group were similar, showing little evidence of specialisation in types of offence.

- Among those with previous convictions, drink drivers were found to have a lower incidence of offending; they had half as many previous convictions as other offenders, and their last court appearance was on average 8 years ago in comparison with an overall average of 3 years.

- Nonetheless, drink drivers were estimated to be twice as likely to have a criminal record as a member of the general population of the same age and gender.

Recent offending of the November 1996 sample

Serious traffic offences were introduced onto the OI in January 1996. The 'recent offending' period of January to November 1996 therefore represents the longest time-span (within our data) for which offenders' previous records include convictions for serious traffic offences. Conviction records over the first ten months of 1996 were therefore analysed for the 21,281 OI sample cases convicted in November 1996. Nearly 31 per cent of the sample had one or more previous convictions in the ten month period (see Figure 4.6). Drink drivers showed the lowest figure at 7 per cent and dangerous drivers the second lowest at 20 per cent. In contrast, 46 per cent of disqualified drivers had recent convictions, and car thieves 48 per cent; both were higher than the 34 per cent for mainstream offenders.

Figure 4.6: **November 1996 OI sample: percentage of offenders with recent convictions (over a ten month period)**

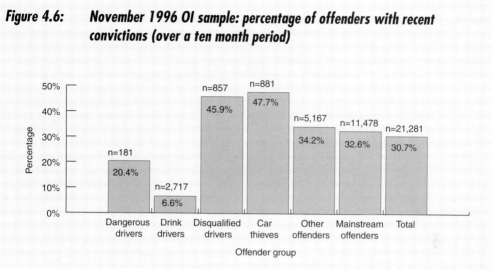

Recent offending: prevalence of offence types

In order to assess specialisation in offence types, we focus on the 6,537 offenders with recent criminal histories only. Table 4.5, which gives the percentage of these offenders with convictions for each of five offence types, shows there were many similarities between the profiles of each offender group, with the highest rate in each case being for mainstream crime. However, there were also clear differences between offender groups, some of which indicated a degree of 'specialisation'. For example, in the ten months 47 per cent of car thieves had previous car theft convictions and 52 per cent of disqualified drivers had convictions for serious traffic offending (the rate for previous disqualified driving alone was 34%).

Table 4.5: *Offenders with recent convictions: the prevalence of each category of previous offence[33]*

	Offender groups						**All**
	Dangerous drivers	Drink drivers	Disqualified drivers	Car thieves	Other offenders	Mainstream offenders	**cases**
Mainstream offences	62.2%	58.7%	53.4%	74.8%	67.9%	81.6%	**75.0%**
Other standard list offences	18.9%	11.2%	16.5%	19.5%	22.4%	14.5%	**17.1%**
Bail breaks or breaches	59.5%	27.9%	35.4%	36.7%	44.2%	38.0%	**39.3%**
Vehicle theft offences	27.0%	3.4%	16.8%	46.7%	12.9%	13.7%	**15.6%**
Serious traffic offences	16.2%	25.7%	52.4%	23.1%	15.5%	10.8%	**15.8%**
Valid n	*37*	*179*	*393*	*420*	*1,769*	*3,739*	**6,537**

Incidence of recent offending

For those with recent convictions, the mean number of court appearances within the ten months was 1.58, with little variation between offender groups – except for the lower figure of 1.23 for drink drivers (See Table 4.6). However, the mean number of recent convictions – 3.43 in the sample as a whole – varied widely between groups, from 1.87 for drink drivers to 4.34 and 4.35 for car thieves and dangerous drivers respectively.[34]

When the breakdown between offence types was simplified (serious traffic offences, car theft and 'mainstream or other' offences) the majority of recent offending was shown to be in the 'mainstream or other' category (see Table 4.6). Even among the two offender groups where previous vehicle-related crime was most common – disqualified drivers and car thieves – nearly two-thirds of offending over the ten months was in this category. Car thieves did, however, have a high rate of previous car theft over that period. To summarise, whilst there was a significant tendency towards specialisation in the recent criminal histories of car thieves and disqualified drivers, this was nonetheless within a broad context of generalised offending. For the other groups of offenders examined, Table 4.6 shows little evidence of specialisation in particular types of offence.

33 November 1996 OI sample. Recent convictions are those in the ten months January to October 1996.
34 Care must be taken in interpreting the figures for dangerous drivers, since there are only 37 who have recent previous convictions.

Table 4.6: **Offenders with recent convictions: the incidence of previous criminality over the ten month period** [35]

Incidence Indicators	Offender groups						All cases
	Dangerous drivers	Drink drivers	Disqualified drivers	Car thieves	Other offenders	Mainstream offenders	
Mean number of previous court appearances	1.65	1.23	1.50	1.59	1.61	1.59	**1.58**
Mean number of previous offences	4.35	1.87	3.05	4.34	3.40	3.45	**3.43**
Mean number of previous serious traffic offence convictions	0.41	0.32	0.82	0.47	0.22	0.16	**0.24**
Mean number of previous vehicle theft convictions	0.70	0.03	0.27	1.07	0.20	0.22	**0.27**
Mean number of previous mainstream and other convictions	3.24	1.51	1.95	2.80	2.98	3.07	**2.92**
Valid n	*37*	*179*	*393*	*420*	*1,769*	*3,739*	**6,537**

Recent convictions for serious traffic offending were evident at significant levels within all offender groups. A total of 1,585 serious traffic offences occurred within the recent criminal histories of the November 1996 sample as a whole. Only 25 per cent (n=397) of these offences were accounted for by the three serious traffic offender groups, with a further 13 per cent (n=199) from the car thieves group. Fully 62 per cent (n=989) appeared within the recent convictions of the 'mainstream' and 'other' groups of offenders (see Figure 4.7). These findings confirmed the relatively low degree of specialisation amongst offender groups.

---

35 November 1996 OI sample. Recent convictions are those in January to October 1996.

Figure 4.7: **Recent convictions for serious traffic offences (previous ten months): the percentage accounted for by each offender group**

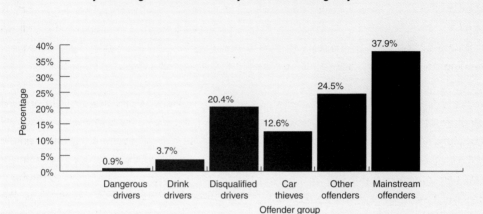

Summary – recent convictions

- *Recent convictions* were assessed over a ten-month period when previous serious traffic offending could be included. 31% of the November 1996 OI sample had been convicted of an offence over the ten months. Drink drivers were the lowest of the offender groups at 7%, followed by dangerous drivers with 20%. 46% of disqualified drivers had a recent conviction.

- For all offender groups, mainstream offences were the most common recent convictions. There was, however, evidence for some degree of specialisation. Among those with previous convictions over the ten months, 47% of car thieves had convictions for car theft and 52% of disqualified drivers had previous serious traffic convictions.

- 62% of the serious traffic convictions in the recent criminal records of the sample as a whole were accounted for by mainstream offenders and other offenders (rather than serious traffic offenders or car thieves), indicating that amongst repeat offenders the extent of specialisation in serious traffic offending was low.

Patterns of 'reconviction'

When the OI data were supplied, the conviction records for offenders were regarded as complete up to mid-1997. For the 21,580 sample cases convicted in March 1996 'follow-up' data were therefore available for some 15 months. This analysis is based on subsequent offending patterns for a twelve month period (up to mid-March 1997).

For the OI data, measures based on subsequent convictions are not straightforward indicators of the likelihood of reconviction in the given period. For example, subsequent convictions can result from offences committed before the 'current' court appearance, simply because of time delays before cases are dealt with in court. The time sequence of a series of court convictions will not be an accurate reflection of the time sequence of offending, especially where an offender is very active (Lloyd et al, 1994: Chapter 2). Nonetheless, the patterns shown by subsequent convictions in the OI data can be used as broad indicators of the level of recorded criminal activity over the twelve month period and the shorthand term 'reconviction' will be used here.[36]

Rates of 'reconviction'

Nearly 34 per cent of the March 1996 sample were convicted again at least once in the follow-up year. The percentage of reconvictions varied considerably between offender groups. Drink drivers showed the lowest rate of reconviction at 11.5 per cent and dangerous drivers the next lowest at 26.5 per cent; the figure for disqualified drivers was 37 per cent, the same as the rate for mainstream offenders. Just over 50 per cent of car thieves were reconvicted in the follow-up year (see Figure 4.8).

---

36 One specific factor likely to have affected subsequent convictions is the imposition of a custodial sentence for the 'current' offence, since offenders are not 'at risk' of further offending when incarcerated. A basic test for the effects of custody was carried out by comparing those given custodial sentences at the current appearance (17% of the sample) with the remaining 83% of offenders, and found that most of the results were, in fact, unchanged. Less obvious is a range of other situations involving periods of custody. For example, an offender may already be in custody at the time of the current court appearance, and will return to custody whatever sentence is given. In fact, points such as these could affect the analysis of previous conviction patterns as well, although it would be very difficult to take account of them.

Figure 4.8: **Percentage of offenders with subsequent convictions (twelve month period): March 1996 OI sample**

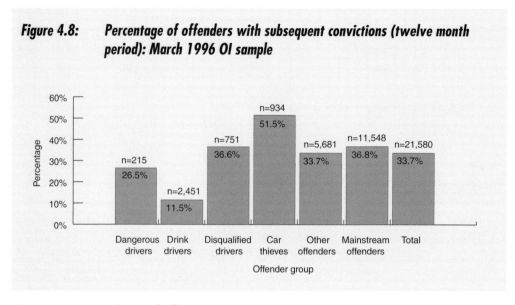

Reconviction: prevalence of offence types

Table 4.7, which is based on the 7,267 're-offenders' only, shows the percentage with subsequent convictions for five main offence types. There were many similarities in the patterns shown by the offender groups; for each group (except drink drivers) the highest rate was for mainstream offences, and the percentage with reconvictions for 'bail breaks and breaches' (mostly breach cases) was around 45 per cent. For the three groups of serious traffic offenders there was clearly some element of 'specialisation' within the reconviction patterns, largely revolving around disqualified driving. Once again, these tendencies towards specialisation occurred within a more general context of non-specialist offending. Further calculations showed that, for serious traffic offenders, 29 per cent of all subsequent offences were for serious traffic offences (predominantly disqualified driving), 8 per cent were for car theft, 20 per cent for 'bail breaks and breaches' and 44 per cent were for mainstream and other offending.[37]

---

37 In many cases disqualification would have been one of the penalties imposed for the sample offence in March 1996, and the reconvictions represent cases where disqualification has been disregarded.

Table 4.7: **Offenders with subsequent convictions: the prevalence of each category of offence (twelve month period)** [38]

	Offender groups						
	Dangerous drivers	Drink drivers	Disqualified drivers	Car thieves	Other offenders	Mainstream offenders	**All cases**
Mainstream offences	57.9%	48.1%	58.2%	74.2%	70.4%	81.2%	**75.5%**
Other standard list offences	12.3%	11.0%	12.7%	17.5%	25.8%	14.7%	**17.6%**
Bail breaks or breaches	43.9%	20.5%	42.2%	44.7%	47.7%	42.9%	**43.4%**
Vehicle theft offences	22.8%	7.4%	16.4%	44.3%	13.4%	13.7%	**15.6%**
Serious traffic offences	38.6%	56.2%	46.5%	31.4%	19.0%	13.6%	**19.3%**
Valid n	57	283	275	481	1,917	4,254	**7,267**

As Table 4.7 indicates, subsequent convictions for serious traffic offences were not confined to specific offender groups. In the whole sample, there were 1,585 serious traffic offence convictions in the twelve months; of these fully 65 per cent stemmed from the 'mainstream offenders' and 'other offenders' groups and 13 per cent from 'car thieves' (see Figure 4.9). Only 22 per cent of serious traffic offence reconvictions in the sample represented repeat offending by the three serious traffic offender groups. Further calculations showed that 73 per cent of these offences (1,687 of the 2,308 total) were for driving whilst disqualified.

---

38 March 1996 OI sample.

Figure 4.9: **Subsequent convictions for serious traffic offences (twelve month period): the percentage accounted for by each offender group**

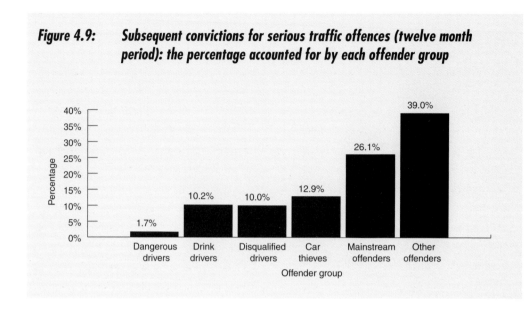

Age and gender

In the sample as a whole, females were significantly less likely to have subsequent offences in the 12 month period (24% for females; 35% for males). Among drink drivers, the 6 per cent reconviction rate for females was lower than the 12 per cent for males; for other serious traffic offenders (and for car thieves) the number of females in the sample was too low to allow a reliable analysis to be made. The age of an offender had a strong effect on the rate for subsequent convictions – the older the offender, the lower the rate of reconviction; with only minor variations, this was found within each of the offender groups (see Appendix A: Table A2).

Summary – subsequent convictions

- Subsequent convictions were assessed over a twelve month period for the March 1996 OI sample. Nearly 34% of offenders were reconvicted in the follow up year. Drink drivers were the least likely to be reconvicted at 11%, compared with 27% of dangerous drivers, 37% of disqualified drivers and 50% of car thieves.

- For each offender group, the most common reconviction was for a mainstream offence; reconvictions for bail breaks or breaches occurred in about 40% of cases where there was subsequent offending.

- For serious traffic offenders, 29% of all reconvictions were for further serious traffic offences (mainly disqualified driving) and 8% were for car theft. The remainder – over 60% – were offences unrelated to vehicle crime.

- In the sample as a whole, 65% of subsequent convictions for serious traffic offences were accounted for by mainstream offenders and other offenders, 13% by car thieves and 22% by serious traffic offenders.

- These results provide further confirmation that although there was some specialisation in repeat serious traffic offending, it was within a context of generalised patterns of offending in criminal histories.

Previous criminal histories and subsequent offending

The criminal history of an offender has a very clear effect on the likelihood of reconviction. For the whole sample, reconviction rates rose from 15 per cent for first offenders, to 34 per cent for those with up to nine previous offences, to 56 per cent for offenders with ten or more previous offences. Each offender group showed rapid increases between first time offenders and prolific offenders. Car thieves had reconviction rates that were higher in each category compared to other offender groups: 31 per cent of first offenders were reconvicted over the twelve month period and the figures rose to 72 per cent for offenders with ten or more previous offences. In sharp contrast, the figures for drink drivers were significantly lower than for other offender groups (see Figure 4.10).

Further analysis was undertaken to understand more completely the effects of previous record and offender group on likelihood of reconviction. The effects of sex, age and custodial sentence were also incorporated into this analysis.[39] The findings were:

---

39 The results summarised here were based on a series of logistic regression analyses. This statistical model had the advantage that the effects of several relevant factors - in this case sex, age and custodial sentence - could be examined together, resulting in estimates of the net effect of each factor (that is, other factors were taken as 'being equal'). Logistic regression has been used very commonly in criminology, where outcome variables are often dichotomous; studies of reconviction are one particular area of application (for example, Lloyd et al , 1994: 33-35, and Appendix D).

- For *overall rates of subsequent conviction*, previous offending has the greatest effect, with age a close second. Persistent offenders under 25 showed especially high rates of reconviction.

- As regards offender groups, car thieves had significantly higher reconviction rates than other groups, whereas drink drivers showed lower rates. Females had slightly lower rates than males.

These comments generally confirmed the analysis based on Figure 4.10.[40]

Figure 4.10: **Reconviction rate, by number of previous offences committed and offender group**[41]

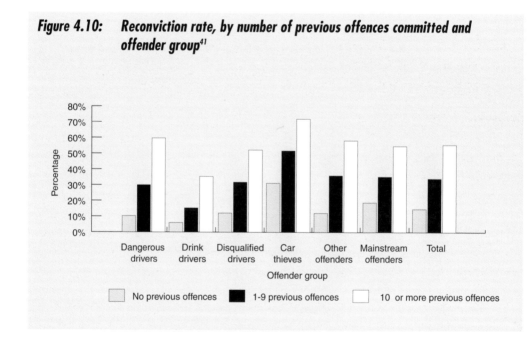

40 Surprisingly, custodial sentence was found to have a negligible effect; as custody reduces the time 'at risk' of offending, it had seemed likely that reconviction rates would also be lower for these cases, but in practice this was not so. However, it should be noted that some 70% of custody cases receive a sentence of 6 months or less. Since in most circumstances prisoners serve a term of about half the stated sentence (Walker and Hough, 1998) these 70% will probably be 'at risk' of further offending for at least nine months in the follow-up period.

41 March 1996 OI sample.

Summary

- The rate of reconviction for first time offenders was found to be 15%, in comparison to 34% for those with up to nine offences and 56% for offenders with 10 or more previous offences.

- Previous offending and age were found to have the greatest effect on overall rates of subsequent conviction. Females had slightly lower rates of reconviction than males.

- Car thieves had significantly higher reconviction rates than other groups, whereas drink drivers showed lower rates; there were no other significant differences between offender groups.

Dangerous driving

On most of the indicators within the OI data, dangerous drivers fell somewhere between disqualified drivers and drink drivers. For example, just over 50 per cent had a previous conviction (less than any other group except drink drivers), and where offenders had a previous record it was slightly less substantial than for disqualified drivers. While the 'profiles' drawn for drink drivers and disqualified drivers have been fairly clear, dangerous drivers consistently seemed to occupy an 'intermediate' position; possibly they were a more heterogeneous group than other serious traffic offenders.

In an exploratory analysis, the 396 dangerous drivers in the total OI sample were separated into three groups: 120 with a previous conviction for car theft, 84 with previous convictions (but none for car theft), and 192 with no previous convictions. The first two groups were fairly similar in gender balance (with only one female in each group), but were otherwise quite different (see Table 4.8). Those with a car theft record were:

- much more likely to be below 21 years of age;
- almost twice as likely to have secondary convictions at the current appearance;
- over twice as likely to have had a first conviction at age less than 16;
- their mean time since last conviction was 31 months, compared with 64 months for those with no car theft in their previous record; and
- they had over twice as many court appearances and offences in their previous records.

To summarise, dangerous drivers with a car theft among their previous convictions showed substantially more criminality on all indicators; their profile was in many respects close to that of disqualified drivers with previous records (compare with Table 4.3). By contrast, the profile for dangerous drivers with a previous record but no car theft showed similarities to that of drink drivers with previous convictions.

Table 4.8: *Dangerous drivers: shown by whether previous convictions include car theft*

	Female	Age 10-20	More than one conviction at current appearance	Convicted before age 16	Mean months since last court appearance	Mean appearances in previous record	Mean offences in previous record	N
Car theft in previous record	0.8%	31.7%	75.0%	54.2%	31.1	7.9	17.9	122
Previous record, but no car theft	1.2%	13.1%	41.7%	23.8%	63.4	3.6	6.5	82

Although this exploratory 'subdivision' of dangerous drivers does not constitute a definitive grouping, it does demonstrate that involvement with car-theft was a very important factor. There are indications that those convicted of dangerous driving may be a mixture of 'driving offenders' and 'dishonest offenders', to use Steer and Carr-Hill's (1967) terms.

YPAC survey

The YPAC survey also highlights the relationships between serious traffic offending and mainstream offending (including drug use). Fifty seven percent of young males who admitted traffic offences in the last year also admitted current mainstream offending, compared with a figure of only 21 per cent for those reporting no current traffic offending (see Table 4.9). For females the reported rates of current mainstream offending were 26 per cent for current traffic offenders compared with 10 per cent for those admitting no current traffic offending. This clear positive association between serious traffic offending and mainstream offending, based on reports of behaviour in the last year, was also evident when examining rates for cumulative participation ('ever' offended).

There were similar findings for reported drug use (see Table 4.9). Forty six percent of current female traffic offenders admitted drug use in the last year, with the comparable figure being only 16 per cent for those reporting no current traffic offending. The rates for male reported drug use in the last year were 55 per cent for current traffic offenders compared with 32 per cent for those not reporting traffic offences. The figures for cumulative participation in drug use and serious traffic offending confirmed a strong positive association between the two reported behaviours for young people of both sexes.[42]

Table 4.9: *Mainstream offending and drug use among young people: traffic offenders compared with non-offenders (YPAC survey)*

	Male Any traffic offences in the last year?		Female Any traffic offences in the last year?	
	No	Yes	No	Yes
All offences in the *last year* (excluding traffic and drug offences)	20.7% n=438	56.9% n=100	9.7% n=659	25.5% n=51
All offences *ever* (excluding traffic and drug offences)	50.3% n=481	78.4% n=105	29.7% n=694	50.5% n=53
Taken drugs in the *last year*	32.4% n=479	54.8% n=104	16.0% n=693	46.2% n=52
Taken drugs *ever*	49.1% n=479	69.6% n=104	26.8% n=693	61.0% n=52

A closer examination of the YPAC data also suggested differences between males and females in the way that mainstream offending and reported drug use were associated with serious traffic offending. Additionally, the two factors may have been of differential importance for particular types of traffic offending. In order to investigate these possibilities, further analyses were carried out to test for the simultaneous effect of several factors (mainstream offending, drug use and access to vehicle) on serious traffic offending in the last year, and also for the three separate traffic offences. Further details are given in Appendix B (Table B3).[43] The results are summarised below.

---

42 Serious traffic offending was also found to be related to alcohol use. This was especially so for females, where 11% of traffic offenders in the last year also admitted heavy drinking; the comparable rate for those reporting no traffic offences was 4%.

43 The statistical method used was logistic regression.

- For males, mainstream offending was found to be more than twice as important as drug use as a determinant of serious traffic offending.
- For females the effects of drug use and mainstream offending on serious traffic offending were of similar weight.

When the separate traffic offences were considered, some more detailed results emerged:

Licence and insurance offences. Within the YPAC survey, this is the traffic offence that most clearly involves dishonesty, and is therefore hypothesised to be the most closely related to mainstream criminality (see section 1). For males, licence and insurance offending was closely related to mainstream offending, with no significant effect shown for drug use, whereas for females mainstream offending and drug use were of about the same importance.[44]

Drink driving. For males, there was slightly more association with drug use than with mainstream offending; for females, drink driving was not related to drug use or mainstream offending. Compared to other serious traffic offences, drink driving was therefore related less closely to mainstream criminality – a finding that echoes the findings from the OI data.

Dangerous driving. For young males and dangerous driving[45], the association with mainstream offending was stronger than that for drug use. Although it could be regarded as a 'driving offence' (Steer and Carr-Hill, 1967) rather than an offence involving dishonesty, as with the OI findings, there was quite a strong association with mainstream crime.

Overall, the YPAC survey therefore confirmed several of the main findings from the OI data concerning the links between serious traffic offending and mainstream offending; it has also allowed the links with drug use to be investigated in more detail. The OI findings on the differences between types of serious traffic offence (especially regarding drink drivers) were also confirmed. In addition, the YPAC data clearly showed the differences between young males and young females in how serious traffic offending is intertwined with mainstream offending and drug use. Further confirmation of these patterns (including gender differences) was also found from the analysis of 'adverse factors', which showed how family, school and peer group factors were differentially associated with mainstream offending and serious traffic offending (see Appendix B).

---

44 Access to a vehicle had a small but positive effect on the rate of licence and insurance offending for males, whereas for females it had no effect. This suggests that when young men obtain a vehicle for their own use, they are more likely than young women to overlook the requirements of tax and insurance.
45 The number of females reporting dangerous driving was too small for analysis.

Summary – YPAC

- For young people – both male and female – there was a clear positive association between serious traffic offending and mainstream offending. For example, 57% of males who admitted traffic offences in the last year also reported current mainstream offending, compared with only 21% for those reporting no current traffic offending.

- For females, drug use was as important as mainstream offending in its association with serious traffic offences. For males mainstream offending was more than twice as important than drug use as an indicator of serious traffic offences.

- The links with mainstream crime and drug use differed between types of serious traffic offence. For males, drink driving offences were more closely related to drug use than to mainstream offending, whereas licence and insurance offending was linked to mainstream crime but not to drug use.

Summary

- The OI data showed there are clear differences between the criminal histories of the three serious traffic offender groups, especially when compared to mainstream offenders.

Drink drivers

- 40% of drink drivers had a criminal record - lower than for any other group of offenders.

- When drink drivers did have a criminal record, it was less extensive than for other groups of offenders. The average time since a last court appearance was 8 years, and less than 12% had a subsequent conviction within a year.

- Drink drivers were approximately twice as likely as the general population to have a criminal record. This finding applied to both males and females, between the ages of 21 and 32.

Disqualified drivers

- Disqualified drivers showed a strong similarity to mainstream offenders.

- Seventy-nine percent had a criminal record (compared with 72% for mainstream offenders). Their level of previous criminality was marginally higher, and they were equally likely to be reconvicted within a year.

- They had a tendency to repeat disqualified driving, but within a context of more generalised offending.

Dangerous drivers

- The criminal histories of dangerous drivers fell somewhere between disqualified drivers and drink drivers. Approximately 50% had a previous conviction, and 26.5% were reconvicted within a year.

- There is evidence that dangerous drivers were a more heterogeneous group than drink drivers or disqualified drivers. About 30% had a previous conviction for car theft, and this group had similar criminal histories to disqualified drivers with previous records. Those without any involvement with car theft showed more similarity to drink drivers.

Young people and serious traffic offending

- The YPAC survey confirmed many of the findings from the OI analysis, particularly the associations of mainstream offending with serious traffic offending.

To broaden the picture of serious traffic offenders and their criminal histories, interviews were undertaken to examine the policing of incidents involving serious traffic offences. The main aim was to ascertain how groups of offences might be discovered or detected as the result of a single incident. The sample of incidents was based on 132 interviews with traffic police in three county forces, designated as 'A' 'B' and 'C' (Appendix C provides the schedule for the interviews carried out). At the time of the research each of the forces had the responsibility of policing a substantial section of motorway as well as the general network of roads. Two forces had a specialised Motorway Unit, with other road policing devolved to divisional level; the third force operated a unified traffic department for the whole force area.

The interview revolved around asking the respondent to recall 'the most recent incident where you have been the officer in the case[46] [and] ... that resulted in a conviction' for each of four types of offence:

- drink driving;
- driving whilst disqualified;
- dangerous or reckless driving; and
- a criminal offence arising from a traffic incident.

Early in the research it emerged that the 'officer in the case' did not always know whether the offender had been convicted, or the exact charge when the case went to court. This situation arose most frequently for dangerous or reckless driving. Reasons for this uncertainty included: the Crown Prosecution Service (CPS) reducing the charge to a lesser offence and the offender pleading guilty; the case being handed over to another force (as with a pursuit that originates in an adjacent force's territory); and, a recent incident not yet dealt with in court.[47]

---

46 The 'officer in the case' took formal responsibility for the incident; this terminology avoids the possibility that the same incident would be offered by two or more respondents.

47 In general, reports of 'borderline' incidents of this kind were accepted unless they clearly fell outside the scope of the study, although a subsequent assessment was made of the 'validity' of each incident report. In general, recent incidents not yet resulting in a conviction were included only if the officer could not offer a valid case for that offence.

Incidents of drink driving and disqualified driving were the most clear-cut, since the evidence involved for these offences (breath-test or disqualification) is usually clear. Incidents of dangerous or reckless driving were sometimes construed more broadly, mainly for the reasons listed above. The question regarding 'a criminal offence arising from a traffic incident' was included in order to give an additional perspective on the connections between mainstream crime and road policing.

Incidents and offences

In general, the findings are based on data from the three forces combined together. Some attention is given to broad comparisons between the forces at a later stage of the interpretation. Incidents where the officer was uncertain of the outcome were classified as 'borderline' cases. These were coded separately, so they could be omitted from the main analysis, but for some purposes they were an important part of the data (especially for crime incidents). Table 5.1 shows the breakdown of incidents, including numbers of borderline incidents and also cases where respondents could not recall relevant incidents.

Table 5.1:   Incidents reported by the interview sample

	Dangerous driving	Drink driving	Disqualified driving	Criminal offence
Valid case	106	125	122	94
Borderline case	6	3	2	16
No incident given	20	4	8	22
Total	132	132	132	132

Timing of incidents

The incidents reported by officers were not always recent events. Although 46 per cent had occurred within the last three months, in 22 per cent of cases it was over a year since the incident. The average time since dealing with a case of dangerous driving was 14.4 months compared with 7.2 months for disqualified driving, 5.8 months for a criminal offence and 4.2 months for drink driving. These figures are mean values based on the sample of 106 officers who were 'fully operational'.[48] The four incident types clearly occurred with different frequencies, with dangerous driving the least common and drink driving the most common. Of course, the most recent incidents dealt with by officers may not have reached court by the time of interview, and would therefore

---

48 See Appendix C, Table C1 for a breakdown of the sample of officers.

be omitted from the sample. Yet the impression was that for most officers these events occur regularly, but not on a daily (or even weekly) basis.

'Simple' and 'complex' incidents

Figure 5.1:   Percentage of 'simple' and 'complex' incidents, by main offence type

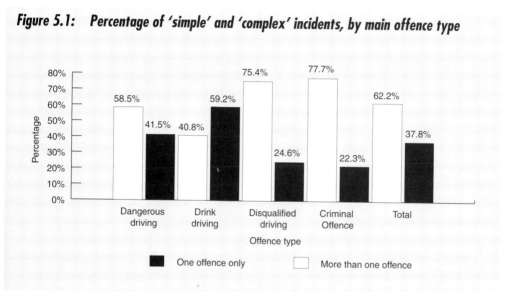

A traffic incident can lead to the discovery of either just one offence or a group of offences. As Figure 5.1 shows, some 38 per cent of incidents were 'simple' (resulting in just one offence conviction) whereas in 62 per cent of cases two or more offences were involved in a 'complex' incident.

The proportion of complex incidents varied considerably. The lowest figure was for drink driving with only 41 per cent involving more than one offence. The highest percentages were for disqualified driving (75%) and incidents involving a criminal offence (78%). Unsurprisingly, the most common kind of additional offences ('secondary offences') were minor traffic offences – including licence and insurance offences, those falling under the heading of 'construction and use' and the flouting of regulations involving commercial vehicles. Over 60 per cent of the 278 complex incidents involved one or more such offences. The number of minor traffic offences was, in fact, greater than for all other secondary offences taken together. For the 278 complex incidents, the mean number of minor traffic offences was 1.17, with little difference between the four incident types. The mean number of other secondary offences varied, with 0.31 for drink driving, 0.70 for disqualified driving, 1.06 for dangerous driving and 1.10 for incidents involving crime.

Table 5.2 shows the breakdown of additional offences by main offence type. The low rates of secondary offending for drink drivers shown in section 4 were supported by this analysis. For dangerous driving and disqualified driving, nearly 20 per cent of cases involved further serious traffic offences, and in some 15 per cent there were convictions for other mainstream offences. Secondary offences of car theft (which included theft of vehicle parts) were most likely to occur for crime or dangerous driving incidents (some 14%). Overall, there was a great deal of consistency between the patterns of secondary offending for serious traffic offending incidents and the OI findings on current convictions in section 4. This suggests that secondary convictions at a given court appearance were very likely to arise from the policing of an individual traffic incident (rather than from other events).

Table 5.2: **The percentage of incidents that included each type of secondary offence**

	Dangerous driving	Drink driving	Disqualified driving	Criminal offence	All valid incidents
Other serious traffic offences	19.8%	10.4%	18.0%	17.0%	16.1%
Mainstream offences (excluding drug and vehicle offences)	14.2%	2.4%	16.4%	36.2%	16.1%
Drug offences	0.0%	0.0%	3.3%	3.2%	1.6%
Car theft	13.2%	0.0%	8.2%	13.8%	8.3%
Minor traffic offences	34.9%	26.4%	50.8%	48.9%	39.8%
Number of incidents	*106*	*125*	*122*	*94*	*447*

Drug offences rarely appeared as secondary offences (see Table 5.2) but they were quite commonly dealt with by traffic officers, since they were the main offence for 19 per cent of the crime incidents (see Figure 5.2). Mainstream offences (such as burglary, theft and violence) accounted for 27 per cent of crime incidents. Other criminal offences were more directly related to vehicle or road policing, including car theft (28%) and traffic-related mainstream crime (11%) which were mainly fraud and forgery relating to vehicles or documents. Overall, just over 50 per cent of the crime cases represented in Figure 5.2 were offences that were not related to traffic or vehicles in a direct way.

Figure 5.2: Crime incidents: main offence types

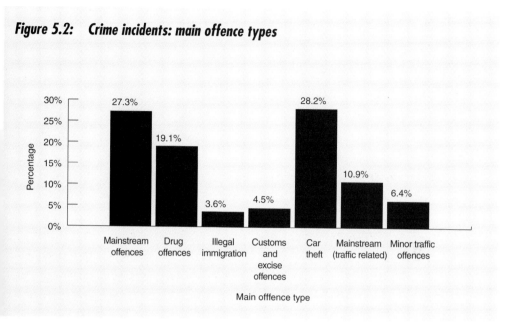

Sequence of events

The sequences of events at the time of incidents are illustrated by cases selected from the sample, using the verbatim accounts given by officers in interviews. As the basis for a more systematic analysis, incidents were coded according to (a) how they arose, and (b) factors mentioned as important in the handling of the incident. For further details see Appendix C (Tables C2 and C3). There were found to be substantial differences between the four incident types, both in the way that incidents originated and the way that officers dealt with them.

- **Drink driving**: Overall, about half the incidents of drink driving arose from routine patrol; in these cases the key factor was often observation of the offender's driving (46% of cases) although some stops were made because of the condition of the vehicle or tax disc. Nearly 40% of cases resulted from 'reactive' work (attending accident scenes or responding to calls from the public), and 7 per cent resulted from specific initiatives. Few drink driving incidents involved follow-up investigations, since the most crucial evidence is provided by the breath test, which is administered in all cases unless it is refused.

Incident 1

"We were patrolling ... and came across a vehicle in middle of the road with its lights on. There was someone unconscious in driver's seat and the engine was running. After shaking him he finally woke up. I called the van out to pick him up. At the station he came round a bit, on the breath machine he blew 69 and 72 ... [about twice the legal limit] ... he admitted to driving and was charged with excess alcohol. He had no previous, he was a security guard, age 34, on the way home – 7 miles away – from a friend's after a nightclub."

(Force A, respondent 13)

Incident 2

"Driver had left the scene of an accident and we traced him. He'd fallen asleep at the wheel, hit the central barrier – he'd pulled over on the hard shoulder and abandoned the vehicle, walked along the hard shoulder ... up to an over bridge and then ... towards his girlfriend's home. He initially denied being involved in the accident but was BT on suspicion, he blew 58 mgs. We [also] reported him for failing to stop at an accident and failing to report an accident ..."

(Force C, respondent 1)

- **Disqualified driving**: Routine stops accounted for the highest number of cases (52%), with offender targeting and 'intelligence-led' together making up a further 24 per cent of incidents. The officer's knowledge about the offender was often the reason for making a routine stop, and in 31 per cent of cases prior information or intelligence was an important factor. Many other factors may be (individually or jointly) the reason for a routine stop, including the condition of the vehicle, the offender's driving or problems with tax discs. Computer checks through PNC (Police National Computer) were also mentioned in 41 per cent of cases, and this was frequently a vital part of the sequence of events at the time of the incident, especially when the officer does not know the offender.[49]

Perhaps the most crucial distinction within disqualified driving incidents was between those where there was prior intelligence on the offender's disqualification (Incident 4) and cases where a routine stop or investigation led on to the discovery that the offender was disqualified (Incidents 3 and 5). Incident 5 also shows quite clearly the way in which the incident itself may need to be followed by the issue of a HORT1 form[50], and a series of subsequent investigations, resulting in charges that cannot be foreseen at the time of the incident itself.

---

49 The percentage of cases involving PNC checks is likely to be higher than 41%, since our coding of factors was based on the officer's account of the incident rather than a 'check-list' of items.

50 A 'HORT1' (Home Office Road Transport) notice requires the driver to produce driving documents at a police station within seven days.

Incident 3

"I saw him driving with no tax disc. He was stopped and he pulled off the main road. When I checked him on PNC I found he was disqualified. He was on a social trip, about 20 miles from home. He was a builder by trade, age 33. He's been to court for it a load of times. His first convictions for disqualified driving were by reason of age. He was different from a lot of offenders because he gave his correct details."

(Force B, respondent 13)

Incident 4

"Information [was received] from a local officer from the estate that the offender was regularly using a motorcycle when banned. We waited for him and when he set off for work we arrested him ...no excise licence... He was disqualified for previous document offences ...couldn't understand that he had to find other alternatives for getting to work."

(Force B, respondent 26)

Incident 5

"[We stopped] a car in poor condition with four people on board ... spoke to driver, asked him to produce via a HORT1. We [then] got called away to a more serious incident ... The driver failed to produce the documents so I went to visit him at home and it was not the same person. The person we visited said "he always gives my details" so we [followed up] the address the second lad had given us. I immediately recognised him and he openly admitted he'd been disqualified. Because he'd previously given false details, I arrested him under Sec. 25 PACE to genuinely establish who he was and he was charged and released ... he was disqualified from totting up [points on a driving licence] ... he had previous for UTMV [car theft]."

(Force C, respondent 33)

- **Dangerous driving**: Incidents fell into four main groups: (a) arising from attendance at accidents (39% in our sample) and where the reconstruction of the events leading up to the accident (through physical evidence and witness reports) will be crucial to the investigation, especially when a fatality or serious injury has occurred; (b) directly observed 'in action' from a patrol car or an unmarked police car (33%) and often needing intervention to stop the vehicle; (c) reported (by the public, through static surveillance or from another force) which are radioed to a patrol for intervention (20%), and (d) complaints from the public that are made retrospectively and then investigated (8%). Incidents 6 to 9 illustrate each group.

Incident 6

"We were at [our base] and member of public rang in with details of accident ... Mercedes saloon into rear of articulated lorry, the saloon car then burst into flames ... Fire brigade were putting out the blaze. There was nobody in the car. The HGV driver said he'd seen someone leaving the scene into adjacent fields. Helicopter and dog patrols attended and we found a man at a telephone kiosk in a village about 2 miles away. He admitted it was his car, he'd been the driver and he smelt strongly of alcohol. He was injured so we took him to P__ hospital ... blood sample came back as 126 (80 is limit)."

(Force C, respondent 2)

Incident 7

"In an unmarked police vehicle I was overtaken by the other vehicle exceeding the speed limit ... [then] he failed to comply with automatic traffic signal ... causing driver of one vehicle to break hard to avoid collision ... joined [motorway] cut straight from slip road to lane one causing others to brake to avoid collision ... finally stopped him at top of slip road ... been out clubbing it he was a sober driver ... I didn't fancy trying to stop a vehicle [earlier] with 4 in the car in bad lighting."

(Force A, respondent 25)

Incident 8

"radioed information ... stolen car that had made off without paying for petrol. A sergeant sighted it and radio came to life. The offender rammed sergeant's car and disabled that car so we took over. There ensued the most horrendous chase that I've ever been involved in. Started off in town 80mph in 30 zones, weaving in and out of cars, wrong side of road on blind bends ... then it went out into the country and ended on the motorway. His driving was so ridiculous that I was the only car that stayed with him ... his speed was excessive 130mph, overtaking on inside ... Then we slowed the traffic with the matrix signs and we were able to later box him ... I've since captured him in 3 more stolen cars ... an extremely persistent car thief."

(Force B, respondent 15)

Incident 9

"reported by the injured party, a road-rage incident ... a young girl was crossing the road, the car approached her at speed narrowly missing her, she swears at him ... having heard her he reversed and came back up the pavement and tried to run her down. He ended up in one garden and she ended up in another having tried to jump out of the way ... we had enough witnesses... he thought he hadn't done anything wrong and thought he was within his rights to teach her a lesson. The offender has no criminal record, only an endorsement."

(Force A, respondent 51)

Criminal Incidents: The sample of 'criminal incidents' largely arose from day-to-day road policing activities, that is: routine or speeding stops (42%), following a report by the public (14%), an observation message (12%), investigating accidents (10%) and investigating a stationary vehicle (7%). In dealing with these cases, officers cited much the same range of factors as for serious traffic offences: the offender's driving, attitude and characteristics, vehicle condition and paperwork, and PNC or computer check were all important in 25 per cent or more cases. Based on further analysis of the data, it was estimated that 20 per cent of incidents resulted from 'proactive' policing, following the targeting of offenders or a planned initiative. The remaining 80 per cent of cases were 'reactive' (resulting from routine stops, radioed information and so on), although intelligence about the offender or the vehicle may have been crucial in how the incident is handled. It is difficult to pick out typical sequences of events, but three examples help to illustrate the variations within this group. Incident 10 shows a drug offence discovered, as the result of the officer following up behavioural cues. For incident 11, it is unlikely that the sequence of events would have happened if the offenders had not run away. By contrast, incident 12 relies on reports from the public; although it was located on the motorway it was not a 'traffic incident' and was therefore categorised as a borderline case for our analysis.[51]

Incident 10	Incident 11
"… suspicion was aroused by the nervousness of the driver. I was on a motorcycle and we all stopped at road works and he was so nervous so we decided to give it a look. He had a boot full of drugs: packets of heroin … he was a courier. It was then passed on to the regional crime squad who had been watching them …"	"We were en route to an accident, and we had to go wrong side of bollards and go around heading towards a car pulling a trailer … the car doors opened, the two occupants … ran away, then we realised the trailer wasn't meant for that vehicle. They'd just pulled away having stolen the trailer … he was wanted on warrant for failing to appear at court … one of the units found the driver that I'd chased and I identified him … we also found a load of tools for going equipped [for stealing]…"
(Force B, respondent 38)	(Force A, respondent 41)

---

51 Other borderline cases included: a hitchhiker found to be wanted on a warrant; someone riding a pedal-cycle on the hard shoulder of a motorway, who had stolen the cycle and a complaint about youths damaging a bus shelter, to which a divisional traffic officer was sent. As the last example illustrates, officers on divisions were sometimes assigned to duty that did not directly stem from traffic policing duties. Responsibility for action stemming from the incident may be 'handed over' to CID or to another force (as in incidents 11 and 12); in these circumstances the traffic officer is less likely to have a complete knowledge of court proceedings and convictions.

Incident 12

"We had a report of a chap hitchhiking ... a driver had put him out on [the motorway] and rang us to say he had a knife ... there had been six or seven calls ... he had no clothes on except a pair of trousers ... he was lying down in the middle of the road, drunk and soaking wet ... he had a Stanley knife. He was aggressive because he'd been drinking and he just slashed at the window with the knife, we told him to put it down, he wouldn't so we got some back up ... he was taken to...hospital and he was known. We then handed it over."

(Force A, respondent 22)

Offenders and vehicles

The distance that offenders travelled from their homes were in general fairly short, although some offenders had travelled very long distances (for example, illegal immigrants from Kosova). Figure 5.3 shows that in over half the cases (55%), the distance travelled was 10 miles or less, with very short journeys of up to four miles common (35%). In only a quarter of cases was the distance in excess of 30 miles. The most surprising feature was the similarity between the patterns of percentages for each incident type; no significant differences were found between the distances travelled by drink drivers, disqualified drivers, dangerous drivers and the criminal offenders. This is not to deny the importance of the more mobile 'travelling criminal' but there seems to be little doubt that for the bulk of the workload of incidents involving serious traffic offences or crime, traffic police were dealing with offenders within a fairly 'local' context.

Figure 5.3:   Incident sample: the distance travelled from home by offenders

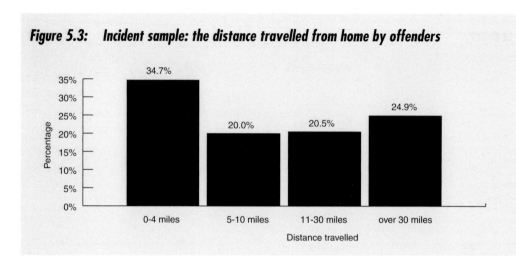

The age and sex of offenders and the type of vehicle were also analysed, showing that:

- The age and sex of offenders in the incident sample reflected the OI findings in most respects. For example: serious traffic offending was seen to be predominantly a male phenomenon, and drink drivers were on average older than other serious traffic offenders. (See Appendix A, Figure A1 for further details)
- Over 80 per cent of the vehicles involved in the incidents were cars, with motorcycles and mopeds only accounting for 3 per cent of cases, and commercial vehicles for 14 per cent.

Differences between forces

Detailed comparisons between the three forces are difficult to make because of the small sample size. The three forces each reported similar proportions of 'complex' incidents (those with secondary offences of some kind). As regards the distance travelled by offenders, Forces A and B had the most 'local' offenders; the distances travelled by offenders in Force C were significantly longer, possibly because of the differences in the motorway systems (and their typical usage) in the three forces. This analysis also confirmed that there was no significant difference between the four types of incident in the distances travelled by offenders; criminal offenders seem to be as likely to be 'local' as serious traffic offenders.

Summary

Road policing and serious traffic incidents

- Although serious traffic incidents occurred regularly, the events were not always recent – 46 per cent of cases occurred within the last three months, but in 22 per cent of cases it was over a year since the incident. Drink driving was the most frequent incident dealt with and dangerous driving the least frequent.

- In over 50 per cent of the crime incidents, the offences were not traffic or vehicle related; they were mainstream crime, including drug offences.

Incidents and offences

- 62 per cent of incidents involved more than one offence. Drink driving incidents were less likely to involve further offences (41%) compared to 75 per cent for disqualified driving incidents.

- Minor traffic offences were the most common secondary offence for all offence groups. However, for dangerous driving and disqualified driving nearly 20 per cent of cases involved further serious traffic offences and 15 per cent involved mainstream offences.

- These results are consistent with findings from the OI (section 4) suggesting that secondary convictions at a given court appearance are very likely to arise from the handling of one traffic incident (rather than from separate policing activities).

Sequence of events

- Routine stops accounted for the highest number of *disqualified driving* cases (52%), and in 31 per cent of cases prior information or intelligence was an important factor.

- About half of *drink driving* incidents arose through routine patrol, and often involved observation of the offender's driving. Nearly 40 per cent resulted from 'reactive' policing involving attendance at accidents or responses to calls from the public.

- *Dangerous driving* incidents arose in a number of ways including attendance at accidents, directly observed 'in action', reported and radioed through for action or complaints from the public investigated retrospectively.

- *Criminal incidents* most commonly arose from routine or speeding stops (42%). Responses to reports from the public, observation messages and investigating accidents together account for over a third of these cases.

Offenders and vehicles

- Offenders were more likely to have travelled only short distances from home when offences were committed, and this was the case across all incident types.

- The age and gender profile of offenders was similar to the national data from the OI (see section 3).

6.   Conclusions and recommendations

The significance of road policing has been enhanced since the Crime and Disorder Act (1998) emphasised the need for local action to address both public safety and crime reduction – the two key features of road policing. This report has investigated the nature of serious traffic offending and the extent to which it is interwoven with mainstream criminal offending. The findings highlight the important role that traffic officers can play in mainstream crime reduction through the enforcement of serious traffic offences. The findings also provide further support to the integration of road policing as a core policing role. The implications of these findings are discussed below and key issues to be taken forward are highlighted.

Profiling serious traffic offenders

Offenders have been separated into three groups (drink drivers, disqualified drivers, and dangerous drivers) for most analyses in this report, but this grouping clearly has limitations, since it is simply based on the 'current' conviction or incident. The grouping has been an invaluable tool for this research, and has enabled important results to be extracted, but as a 'typology' of serious traffic offenders it is a somewhat blunt instrument. However, inferences can be drawn from the findings of this report to provide a general overview of serious traffic offenders.

Serious traffic offenders were found to be predominantly male. The age profiles of dangerous drivers and disqualified drivers were similar to those of mainstream offenders – between 60 per cent and 75 per cent of offenders were in the age-range 18 to 32 years. However, nearly half (48%) of drink drivers were found to be 33 years or older.

The YPAC survey showed 50 per cent of males and 17 per cent of females aged between 21 and 25 reporting *ever* committing a serious traffic offence, confirming the importance of gender. Serious traffic offending was found to be significantly more prevalent amongst young white people, as opposed to other ethnic groups. Young white males were found to be more than three times more likely to have committed a serious traffic offence than young black males. For females, a difference in prevalence was also evident, although not as extreme. The YPAC survey showed that males in higher social class groups were more likely to drink and drive, and suggested that those in lower social groups may be likely to commit licence and insurance offences. Adverse factors relating to family, school and peer group, found to correlate with mainstream offending, were also found to be related to serious traffic offending. This implies that those factors linked to mainstream offending are also indicators of serious traffic offending.

The offending profile of serious traffic offenders can be summarised as follows:

- *Drink drivers* had less extensive criminal records than other groups of serious traffic offenders – only 40 per cent had a criminal record, the average time since their last court appearance was eight years and only 12 per cent had a subsequent conviction within a year.

- *Disqualified drivers* showed a similar offending profile to mainstream criminal offenders. Seventy nine percent had a criminal record (72% for mainstream offenders), their levels of previous offending were slightly higher than for mainstream offenders and they were equally likely to be convicted again within a year (37% were reconvicted).

- Approximately 50 per cent of *dangerous drivers* had a previous conviction and approximately a quarter were reconvicted within a year. Dangerous drivers may be a more varied group of offenders than other serious traffic offenders; about 30% had a previous conviction for car theft, and this group had similar criminal histories to disqualified drivers with previous records. Those without any involvement with car theft showed more similarity to drink drivers.

An important point about a serious traffic offender profile, however, is the level of non-specialisation of offence types – those repeatedly committing serious traffic offences are likely to commit mainstream offences as well. The evidence shows that serious traffic offenders cannot be thought of as otherwise law-abiding members of the public. Even drink drivers (who were less involved in mainstream crime than other serious traffic offenders) were estimated to be twice as likely to have a criminal record as members of the general population. When serious traffic offenders were reconvicted, there was a tendency for repeat serious traffic offending (especially disqualified driving) although this was in a context of more generalised criminal offending.

Points for action

- The findings from this report can be used to provide (albeit rather crudely) profiling of traffic offenders and their offending behaviour. The profiles should not be taken as absolute. However, they can guide and help focus effort when devising strategies to target offenders or offending behaviour through specific initiatives. For example, the report has shown that females are highly unlikely to be convicted of serious traffic offences. Also, the report dispels any preconceptions regarding serious traffic offending and ethnicity. The sample shows that young white males are much more likely to commit serious traffic offences than young black males. They are also more likely to commit these offences than young Asian males. In 1998/9, however, black people were five times more likely to be stopped and searched than whites (Home Office, 1999). Obviously, these figures are for all stop and search incidents, not just those involving vehicles. However, there are still implications for those devising strategies and involved in 'stop and search'. These findings need to be taken into consideration when targeting serious traffic offences and offenders.

- As certain groups of serious traffic offenders are also highly likely to commit mainstream offences, targeting these offenders could help disrupt mainstream crime. Enforcement of serious traffic offences can help to deter and prosecute those also involved in mainstream criminal activity. This could be achieved, for example, by targeting those offenders who continue to drive whilst disqualified. These individuals could be considered to 'self-select' in a similar way to those who illegally park in disabled bays (see Chenery et al 1999). The arrest of an offender for this type of traffic offence could lead to the prevention of other mainstream offences occurring that are perhaps more difficult to detect.

Links with previous research

Although the current research has broken new ground in many respects, there are several areas of consistency with previous work. In particular, Steer and Carr-Hill's (1967) distinction between 'dishonest offenders' and 'driving offenders' finds some support in our data. The 'dishonest' group would include disqualified drivers and those driving without a licence or insurance (the traffic offence most closely linked to mainstream crime within the YPAC data). However, our findings indicate that (at least for the 1990s) Steer and Carr-Hill's 'driving offenders' are not simply members of the general driving population who are 'unlucky' enough to be caught. Drink drivers are estimated to be twice as likely to have a previous record as a member of the general population, and for dangerous and reckless driving there is evidence of connections both with mainstream crime and car theft. These findings suggest that Steer and Carr-Hill's concept of the 'driving offender' is in need of further development, if it is to be consistent with 1990s data.

Farrington's (1994) comments about the low levels of specialisation in offending are broadly supported through analysis of the OI data. Where serious traffic offenders are involved in repeat offending, their criminal histories show a wide variety of offence types. There is a degree of specialisation for serious traffic offending but within a broad context of more general offending, as research by Sugg (1998) also confirms.[52]

Points for action

- Analysis of the criminal careers of minor traffic offenders could provide useful information regarding links with serious traffic offending and mainstream offending. The links may be closest with minor traffic offences that involve dishonesty (see also Chenery *et al*, 1999).

- Re-analysis of the Offenders Index in a few years' time, when there will be a more extensive data source including serious traffic offences, would be a useful exercise. Further evidence on the links between serious traffic offending and mainstream criminal offending – for example the relationship between car theft and dangerous driving – could perhaps enable the development of more sensitive profiles of traffic offenders.

The role of traffic officers and intelligence

Ogilvie-Smith et al (1994) showed a breakdown of how traffic officers spent their time on duty. This showed that 30 per cent of a traffic officer's time was spent dealing with traffic incidents and checks; about 25 per cent of time was devoted to preventative patrol, covering both traffic and crime, and a further 7 per cent was spent on individual crime incidents. The current research integrates with their findings and highlights further the extent to which traffic officers deal with mainstream criminal incidents as well as traffic incidents. Of the criminal incidents examined in this study just over 50 per cent involved offences that were *not* directly vehicle or traffic related.

---

52 Sugg's (1998) study of offenders attending 'motor projects' run by probation services, suggested that '... motoring offenders on these programmes were not specialists, as they had previous convictions for theft (75%), burglary (60%) and offences of violence against the person (30%)' (1998:3).

The report provides information on how incidents arise and the sequence of events at the time of the incident that lead to an arrest. 'Formal' procedures (checks on the vehicle's construction and use, checks with PNC for driver and vehicle, the issuing of HORT1 notices, and breath tests) are all important components of the traffic officer's handling of an incident. However, 'informal' procedures (assessments of the offender's appearance and demeanour, incongruity between the vehicle and its passengers, or simply a feeling that there is 'something not quite right') are also important. Especially in the more complex incidents, it is the mesh between the formal and informal aspects of procedure that shapes the sequence of events.

Due to the distinctiveness of each of the offence types studied, the use of 'formal' and 'informal' procedures varied considerably. The implication is that any policy regarding targeting and detecting serious traffic offenders needs to recognise the different approaches required to combat the different types of traffic offence. For example, disqualified drivers were more often detected through prior intelligence than for other offence types. However, behavioural cues played a significant contribution to detecting all offence types.

Intelligence plays a crucial role in dealing with incidents of all types - sometimes as prior information, but more generally as evidence collated in dealing with the incident (including follow-up investigations after the incident itself). The report indicates the benefits of cross-communication of traffic intelligence and criminal intelligence specifically because traffic officers deal with both traffic and criminal offenders in their routine duty. Offender targeting was often used for disqualified drivers, but was rarely used for the other three incident types. The HMIC thematic inspection report on *Road policing and traffic* (1998) highlights the importance of intelligence-led road policing through the use of a model (Figure 6.1). The model emphasises the need to take into account location, the offender (including their behaviour) and the possible preventative measures when using intelligence to combat both road crime and casualty reduction. Figure 6.1 illustrates this model as an example of the type of strategy that could be used to reduce this type of crime.

Figure 6.1: **An example of an intelligence-led road policing model**

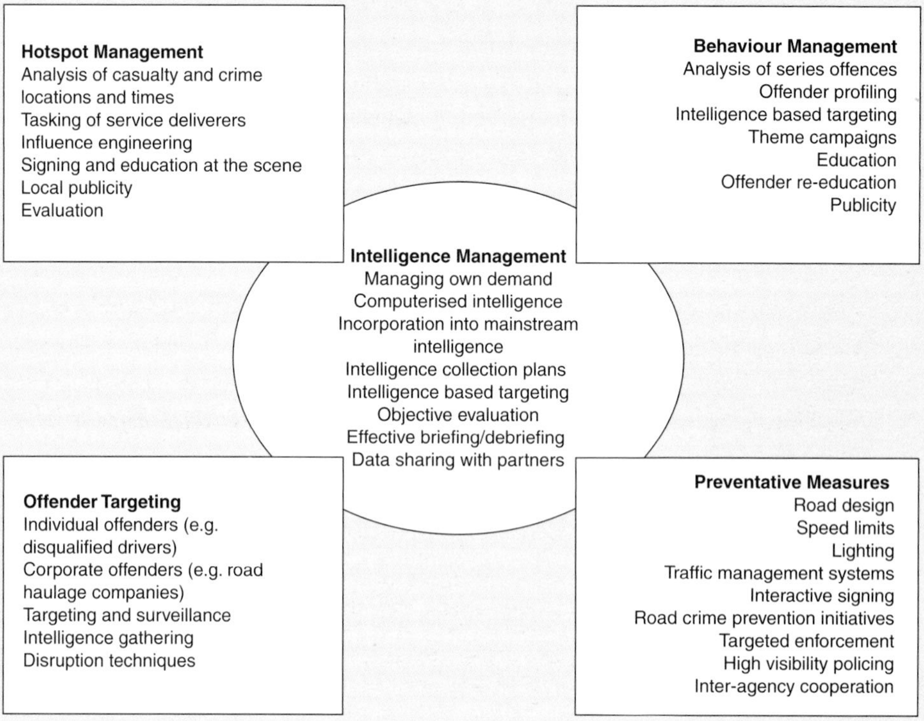

Hotspot Management
Analysis of casualty and crime
locations and times
Tasking of service deliverers
Influence engineering
Signing and education at the scene
Local publicity
Evaluation

Behaviour Management
Analysis of series offences
Offender profiling
Intelligence based targeting
Theme campaigns
Education
Offender re-education
Publicity

Intelligence Management
Managing own demand
Computerised intelligence
Incorporation into mainstream
intelligence
Intelligence collection plans
Intelligence based targeting
Objective evaluation
Effective briefing/debriefing
Data sharing with partners

Offender Targeting
Individual offenders (e.g.
disqualified drivers)
Corporate offenders (e.g. road
haulage companies)
Targeting and surveillance
Intelligence gathering
Disruption techniques

Preventative Measures
Road design
Speed limits
Lighting
Traffic management systems
Interactive signing
Road crime prevention initiatives
Targeted enforcement
High visibility policing
Inter-agency cooperation

Ackroyd *et al* suggest that in the early 1990s their sample of traffic police made better use of IT systems than other parts of the police service (1992:116), and this "... reflected and enhanced the autonomy of officers and the skilful execution of their work ...". Our study of incidents confirmed that traffic officers are crucially reliant on access (via local controllers) to PNC and DVLA records and local databases for checks on both drivers and vehicles. Improvements to the technological tools used by traffic officers could enhance their roles significantly.

Points for action

- The report analyses the role traffic officers play in dealing with both traffic incidents and mainstream crime. The findings highlight the possible impact that traffic officers can have in crime reduction. Many offenders committing serious traffic offences may be involved in mainstream crime. Therefore offenders could be deterred and prevented from committing mainstream crime through the enforcement of serious traffic offences. The findings from this report provide evidence to further enhance the importance of their role as emphasised by ACPO, HMIC and the Government.

- Disqualified drivers have a very close association with mainstream crime with 78 per cent having a previous criminal conviction. However, prior intelligence was found to be used in only half of all arrests. Greater effort could be given to targeting disqualified drivers through the use of intelligence. This could impact significantly on mainstream crime as well as that of serious traffic offences.

- Inter-communication has been shown to be important in combating crime. This could be achieved by local intelligence officers co-ordinating and liaising between traffic officers and uniform/CID branches to improve the flow of 'cross-communication'. As traffic officers deal with a substantial amount of criminal incidents, together with the finding that repeat traffic offenders are likely to commit mainstream offences as well, sharing intelligence could enhance the disruption of crime.

- Improvements could be made to the links and accessibility of information and data sources including DVLA and Phoenix. Other information that could be considered to be linked would be MOT and insurance data. It is important that information on these systems is kept up-to-date so those officers at the road-side can deal efficiently and effectively with both traffic and mainstream criminal incidents. Data quality is also crucial, lending further weight to the recommendations of Russell (1998).

Concluding remarks

This report supports the idea that road policing should be viewed as part of core policing. In the fields of both further research and policing, our findings demonstrate that, in many respects, serious traffic offending should be placed squarely within the definition of 'real crime'.

Table A1: **The grouping of offences for the analysis of the Offenders Index data**

	Principal offence convictions (1996 sample) [5]
Group A: mainstream offences[4]	(23,026)
1. violence against the person	5,569
2. burglary	2,747
3. robbery	520
4. theft and handling stolen goods (not involving motor vehicles)	8,477
5. criminal damage	2,693
6. drug offences	3,020
Group B: other standard list offences[4]	(4,384)
7. sexual offences	605
8. fraud and forgery	1,413
9. standard list offences not classified elsewhere	1,483
10. offence classification not determinable	883
Group C: breach cases and breaking bail	(3,497)
11. failing to surrender to bail	1,814
12. breach cases [3]	1,683
Group Y: vehicle related theft and taking	(1,815)
13. theft and taking of vehicle	919
14. theft from vehicle	390
15. aggravated vehicle taking (indictable)	426
16. aggravated vehicle taking (non-indictable)	80
Group X: serious traffic offences	(7,172)
17. causing death by dangerous driving	28
18. dangerous driving	368
19. driving in excess of the alcohol limit	5,168
20. driving whilst disqualified	1,608
Group Z: motoring offences (non standard list)	(1,223)
21. summary motoring offences (not standard list) *	1,223
Group W: other offences (non standard list)	(1,744)
22. summary non-motoring offences (not standard list) *	1,744
Total	**(42,861)**

Notes

1. A conviction for a standard list offence is the criterion for inclusion in the Offenders Index (OI). The standard list includes all indictable offences and some of the more serious summary offences. From 1996, driving in excess of the alcohol limit, dangerous driving and driving whilst disqualified were added to the list. Convictions for non-standard list offences appear in the OI when they are heard in court with standard list offences. Non-standard list offences are designated by *.

2. Groupings above are based either on individual offence categories or on aggregations of those categories that are used in the OI (and in *Criminal Statistics*).

3. Breach cases are not offences (though the case is often heard with a new offence if one has been committed). Breaches arise from non-compliance with the requirements or conditions of a previous sentence - usually a non-custodial sentence.

4. Group A 'mainstream offences' comprise the main types of indictable crime, where the literature on criminal careers has suggested there is little specialisation. Two of the offences for which some element of specialisation has been found (sexual offences and fraud and forgery) are classified in Group B, which also contains offences that are not within the specified main types of offence, or where the offence classification was not known (a small proportion of these may be non-standard list offences).

5. The counts that appear in this column are for principal offence convictions only; the figures therefore also correspond to the number of offenders for the 1996 sample.

Table A2: Percentage of offenders with subsequent convictions by age

Age (years)	Offender groups						
	Dangerous drivers	Drink drivers	Disqualified drivers	Car thieves	Mainstream offenders	Other	Total
10 to 20	38.2%	16.2%	52.6%	55.2%	46.1%	49.6%	46.9%
	n=55	n=167	n=97	n=591	n=3,178	n=1,228	n=5,856
21 to 25	27.1%	16.7%	41.8%	47.9%	38.3%	37.9%	36.6%
	n=70	n=479	n=239	n=211	n=2,752	n=1,574	n=5,325
26 to 32	24.4%	13.9%	38.4%	40.7%	33.8%	30.8%	30.8%
	n=45	n=599	n=203	n=86	n=2,688	n=1,362	n=4,983
33 or more	13.3%	7.7%	21.7%	41.3%	24.2%	19.2%	19.1%
	n=45	n=1,206	n=212	n=46	n=2,390	n=1,517	n=5,416

Figure A1: *Percentage of male and female offenders: OI sample compared with the traffic incident sample.*

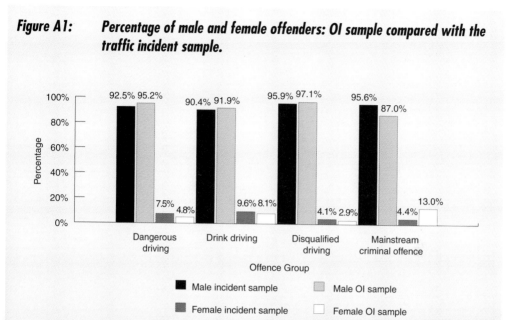

Appendix B: The young people and crime survey

Table B1: Offence items for the young people and crime survey [1]

Traffic offences

1. Driven a car, motor-cycle or moped on a public road without licence and/or insurance.
2. Driven a car, motor-cycle or moped knowing you had drunk more than the legal limit.
3. Driven a car, motor-cycle or moped when you were disqualified from driving by a court.
4. Had an accident when driving a car, motor-cycle or moped, without stopping to see what happened or reporting it to the police.
5. Driven a car, motor-cycle or moped in a dangerous or reckless manner.

Property offences (burglary, theft, handling, fraud etc, not involving motor vehicles)

6. Stolen money from a gas or electricity meter, public telephone, vending machine, video game or fruit machine.
7. Stolen anything from a shop, supermarket, or department store.
8. Stolen anything in school worth more than £5.
9. Stolen anything from the place where you work worth more than £5.
10. Taken away a bicycle without the owner's permission.
11. Pickpocketed anything from anybody.
12. Snatched from a person a purse, bag or something else.
13. Sneaked or broken into a private garden, a house or a building intending to steal something (not meaning abandoned or ruined buildings).
14. Stolen anything worth more than £5, not mentioned already (for example, from a hospital, youth club, sports centre, pub, building site, etc.).
15. Bought, sold or held onto something you knew or believed at the time had been stolen.
16. Sold a cheque book, credit card, cash point card (ATM card) belonging to you or someone else so that they could steal money from a bank account.
17. Used a cheque book, credit card, cash point card (ATM card) which you knew or believed at the time had been stolen to get money out of a bank account.
18. Claimed on an insurance policy, an expenses form, a tax return or a social security benefit form that you knew to be incorrect in order to make money.

Vehicle taking and theft

19 Taken away a motorcycle or moped without the owner's permission.
20 Taken away a car without the owner's permission.
21 Stolen anything out of or from a car.

Offences involving violence

22 Threatened somebody with a weapon or with beating them up, in order to get money or other valuables from them.
23 Participated in fighting or disorder in a group in a public place (for example, football ground, railway station, music festival, riot, demonstration, or just in the streets).
24 Beaten up someone not belonging to your immediate family, to such an extent that you think or know that medical help or a doctor was needed.
25 Beaten up someone belonging to your immediate family, to such an extent that you think or know that medical help or a doctor was needed.
26 Hurt someone with a knife, stick or other weapon.

Offences involving damage

27 Damaged or destroyed, on purpose or recklessly, something belonging to somebody else (for example, telephone box, bus shelter, car, window of a house, etc.).
28 Set fire on purpose or recklessly to something not belonging to you. It might be to paper or furniture, to a barn, a car, a forest, a basement, a building or something else.
29 Writing or spraying on walls, buses, train seats, shelters etc.

Notes:
1. In addition to the 29 offences listed above, respondents were asked about four other offences: travelled on a bus, train or underground without paying your fare; stealing something from home/place of living worth more than £5; carrying a weapon, such as a knife, stick etc. to defend yourself or to attack other people; and, threatening someone for any other reason (other than item 22).
2. For each item, respondents were asked whether they had ever done this, and if so for an estimate of how many times; they were then asked the same questions relating to the last year (i.e.1992).
3. The order in which the items were presented was the same for all respondents, but does not correspond to that given above.

Table B2: *Traffic offending and socio-economic status: the percentage of males admitting each type of offence* [1]

	Socio-economic status				All cases
	I/II (AB)	IIINM (C1)	IIIM (C2)	IV/V (DE)	
Offending 'ever'?					
Any serious traffic offence	39.5%	41.3%	43.4%	38.2%	40.7%
Licence or insurance offence	24.5%	24.8%	34.9%	35.1%	30.7%
Drink driving	25.6%	15.3%	15.0%	11.4%	17.1%
Dangerous driving	25.0%	27.0%	16.7%	18.0%	20.5%
Offending in the 'last year'?					
Any serious traffic offence	30.4%	14.7%	22.0%	15.5%	22.0%
Licence or insurance offence	13.5%	12.1%	14.1%	13.6%	13.6%
Drink driving	20.6%	5.0%	7.1%	3.5%	9.8%
Dangerous driving	12.1%	8.7%	7.7%	6.2%	8.7%
Unweighted N	*114*	*57*	*249*	*158*	*578*

1   YPAC, core sample; weighted estimates of percentages.

Table B3: *The joint effects of mainstream offending and drug use on serious traffic offending in the last year: partial correlations.* [1]

Offending in 'last year'?	Mainstream offending in last year?	Drug use in last year?	Access to vehicle in last year?
Males			
Licence or insurance offence	0.30	–	0.12
Drink driving	0.17	0.21	0.24
Dangerous driving	0.24	0.09	0.22
Any serious traffic offence	0.23	0.09	0.24
Females			
Licence or insurance offence	0.16	0.15	–
Drink driving	–	–	0.22
Any serious traffic offence	0.17	0.15	0.21

1. Core sample: 617 males, 775 females. Results are based on a series of logistic regression analyses, with the data unweighted. Each row of the table shows the dependent variable (for a given regression) and independent variables are shown in the three columns. All figures are estimated partial correlation coefficients in the final equation (after omitting non-significant effects) and are therefore statistically significant at (at least) the 5 per cent level. The analysis also tested for the effects of weighting by including the reweighting variable as an independent variable; it was found to be non significant in each regression.

Table B4: Young people and crime: the effect of adverse factors on serious traffic offending and on mainstream offending [1,2]

	Number of adverse factors					All cases	Measure of association (gamma) [3]
	none	one	two	three	four		
Males							
'Ever' commit a serious traffic offence?	16.0%	31.0%	55.9%	48.8%	79.0%	41.8%	G = 0.46
'Ever' commit a mainstream offence?	29.2%	43.9%	70.0%	73.4%	80.2%	56.6%	G = 0.50
Unweighted N	101	168	153	117	49	588	
Females							
'Ever' commit a serious traffic offence?	10.2%	10.1%	18.0%	23.8%	27.0%	15.4%	G = 0.31
'Ever' commit a mainstream offence?	17.3%	22.2%	35.4%	48.0%	66.2%	31.4%	G = 0.44
Unweighted N	146	188	188	153	84	747	

1. Total sample, age 16 and over: weighted percentages.
2. Note that the percentages shown for mainstream offending differ from those in Graham and Bowling (1995: Tables 4.6 and 4.7) for two main reasons. First, only respondents aged 16 and over are included here. Second, Graham and Bowling base their analysis on a specific set of more serious criminal offences, rather than all mainstream offending.
3. The Gamma values (G) shown measure the association between the dependent variable (for example 'ever commit a serious traffic offence?') and adverse factor score.

Appendix C:

Interviews of officers involved in traffic policing

Schedule for interviews

1. Data on the individual officer: force, division or unit, age-group, sex, rank, years of police service, years in traffic policing.

2. For the purposes of this research we are interested in your experience of incidents - mainly those involving serious traffic offences. For each type of offence we want to ask about the most recent incident where you have been the officer in the case. We are interested in incidents that, as far as you know, resulted in a conviction.

   - driving whilst disqualified;
   - drink driving;
   - a criminal offence arising from a traffic incident; and
   - dangerous or reckless driving.

3. For each incident (after identifying the most recent incident involving the relevant offence).

   - When was this? And in what location?
   - How did this incident arise?
   - Was there anything else that led up to the incident or your involvement?
   - Could you tell me about the sequence of events at the time. (If multiple offences, which came to light first? If single offence only, what led you to conclude the incident?).
   - Did offences of any other kind result from dealing with this incident?
   - What type of vehicle was involved?
   - Now, about the offender: male or female? Age?
   - Was he or she local to the area, or from outside the area?
   - Do you know what type of journey they were taking? (Estimate of distance from offender's home if possible).
   - Was there anything about the offender, the vehicle, the information you had or the incident itself that led you to handle the situation as you did?

4. General comments about the topics covered by the research.

Table C1: Sample of traffic officers interviewed

	Force A	Force Force B	Force C[3]	Table total
Division or unit				
Motorway unit	34	-	20	54
Division[1]	15	-	14	29
Unified	-	49	-	49
Officer age				
Up to 39 years	27	29	16	72
40 years or more	22	20	18	60
Rank of officer				
Constable	42	42	33	117
Sergeant	6	6	1	13
Inspector and above	1	1	-	2
Currently operational?[2]				
Fully operational	34	39	33	106
Mostly operational	3	-	1	4
Specialist	1	3	-	4
Supervisory/intelligence	11	7	-	18

Notes
1. In Force A, officers were interviewed on three Divisions, all of which were relatively small. In Force C, one large Division was included.
2. 'Supervisory and intelligence' includes supervisors on each of the three divisions in Force A and local intelligence officers. 'Specialist' includes accident investigation officers.
3. In Force C, because of time constraints, interviews were confined to operational officers.

Table C2: How the incident arose, by type of incident

How incident arose	Dangerous driving	Drink driving	Disqualified driving	Criminal offence	Notes [1]
Response to accident	40%	21%	5%	10%	Usually called via radio, but sometimes patrols just come across an accident. Initial reports are mainly by member of public
Routine stop	22%	33%	51%	39%	For lights, vehicle condition, out of date tax disc and so on. Often based on behavioural cues by driver or passengers
Speeding stop	4%	8%	7%	3%	For speeding that is directly observed
Stationary vehicle	1%	8%	2.5%	7%	Routine patrol investigates stationary vehicle (mainly breakdowns)
Initiative	–	7%	2.5%	3%	Includes planned program of stops (e.g. crackdown on post-pub drivers)
Multi-agency	–	–	1%	3%	With MOT, DSS, Customs & Excise
Observation message	11%	–	–	12%	Radio call on specified vehicle (may be stolen) - source often other police area or force; tracker signal
Report from public	18%	19%	4%	14%	Usually phoned in, and radioed out; includes calls from workers in shops, offices, service stations. (Excludes reports of accidents)
Offender targeting	1%	1%	17%	–	Specific offender (or group) targeted, based on prior information/intelligence
Intelligence based	1%	2%	7%	4%	Stop of known individual (esp. disqualified driver)
Other	3%	1%	3%	4%	Other (or not known)
No. of cases	102	124	121	94	

1.   Notes cover the most frequent examples, but are not exhaustive of the category.

Table C3: **Factors mentioned as important in the investigation, by type of incident[1]**

Factor	Dangerous driving	Drink driving	Disqualified driving	Criminal offence	Notes and common examples[3]
Offender's driving	49%	46%	29%	28%	Weaving about; no seat belt;speed etc.(only coded when driving was directly observed)
Offender's attitude or demeanour	25%	19%	20%	34%	Uncomfortable; not looking in the eye; 'something not quite right' (includes passengers and accomplices)
Offender's characteristics	9%	4%	16%	26%	'Scruffy'; tattooed; 'four lads in a battered car' etc.
Vehicle condition	10%	10%	30%	27%	Tyres; lights; overloaded; 'tatty' vehicle; 'construction & use' generally
Vehicle paperwork	11%	10%	57%	35%	Tax disc; HORT1 check. Also commercial regulations (tachometer etc.)
Incongruity of factors	2%	4%	3%	13%	Mismatch of vehicles & occupants; 'not feel right'
Radioed information	43%	27%	9%	29%	Information or complaint from public to own (or another) force, relayed via radio
Prior information, intelligence	5%	7%	31%	24%	Observation message on vehicle (including stolen); targeting likely offender
Circumstances at accident	43%	25%	7%	10%	(Only when accident attended)
Breath test (including refused)	18%	100%	15%	3%	Including those shown to be negative
PNC or other computer check[2]	9%	4%	41%	25%	Including PNC check on stolen vehicles/plates
Road block	4%	–	–	2%	All varieties including 'Stinger' and TPAC (excludes road blocks set up for an initiative)
Pursuit and stop	24%	1%	7%	7%	Pursuit of offender trying to get away by car, and stop (possibly TPAC)
Other	19%	10%	7%	43%	Other important factor
No. of cases	*106*	*125*	*122*	*94*	

Notes
1. All factors are coded, and there is no upper limit to the number of factors coded for any one incident. In general, the percentages in the table should be regarded as a set of minimal estimates, since the coding is based on the officer's verbatim account of the incident rather than a 'check-list' of items.
2. This factor is underestimated here; in many cases it was not mentioned by officers, although PNC or local computer data-bases would necessarily have been utilised.
3. Explanation of terms. A 'HORT1' (Home Office Road Transport) notice, issued by the traffic officer, requires the driver to produce their driving documents relating to the vehicle, at a police station within seven days. TPAC (Tactical Pursuit and Containment) is a nationally agreed set of approved procedures for pursuing and stopping vehicles. PNC is the Police National Computer. The 'Stinger' is a portable device for puncturing the tyres of a moving vehicle.

Table C4: Offender's distance from home, by type of incident

| | Incident type | | | | |
	Dangerous driving (%)	Drink driving (%)	Disqualified driving (%)	Criminal offence (%)	All incidents (%)
Up to 4 miles	29.4	35.0	38.8	34.8	34.7
5 to 10 miles	24.5	22.8	18.1	13.5	20.0
11 to 30 miles	22.5	20.3	19.8	19.1	20.5
Over 30 miles	23.5	22.0	23.8	32.6	24.9
No. incidents	*102*	*123*	*116*	*89*	*430*

References

Ackroyd, S., Harper, R., Hughes, J.A., Shapiro, D. and Soothill, K. (1992) *New Technology and Practical Police Work.* Buckingham: Open University Press.

ACPO Traffic Committee (1997) *Effective Road Policing: Management Handbook, Vol 1.* London: Association of Chief Police Officers.

ACPO Traffic Committee (1998) *National Road Policing Strategy* London: Association of Chief Police Officers.

Blumstein, A., Cohen, J., Roth, J.A. and Visher, C.A. (1986) *Criminal Careers and Career Criminals, Vol 1.* Washington, D.C.:National Academy Press.

Chenery, S., Henshaw, C. and Pease, K. (1999) *Illegal Parking in Disabled Bays: A Means of Offender Targetting.* London: Home Office, Policing and Reducing Crime Unit, Briefing Note 1/99.

Dix, M.C. and Layzell, A.D. (1983) *Road users and the police.* London: Croon Helm.

Farrington, D. (1994) 'Human development and criminal careers' in M. Maguire, R. Morgan and R. Reiner, eds. *The Oxford Handbook of Criminology.* Oxford: Oxford University Press.

Graham J. and Bowling B. (1995) *Young People and Crime.* Home Office Research Study 145. London: Home Office.

Her Majesty's Inspector of Constabulary (1998) *Road Policing and Traffic: HMIC Thematic Inspection Report.* London: The Stationery Office Group Ltd.

Home Office (1998a) *Criminal Statistics, England and Wales, 1997.* London: HMSO.

Home Office (1998b) *Motoring Offences, England and Wales, 1996.* Home Office Statistical Bulletin, Issue 8/98. Home Office: Research and Statistics Directorate.

Joslin, P. (1994) 'Traffic and crime go together'. *Police.* 25(6):18.

Light, R., Nee, C. and Ingham, H. (1993) *Car Theft: the Offender's Perspective.* Home Office Research Study No. 130. London: HMSO.

Lloyd, C., Mair, G. and Hough, M. (1994) *Explaining Reconviction Rates: a Critical Analysis.* Home Office Research Study No. 136. London: HMSO.

Macmillan, J. (1975) *Deviant Drivers.* Farnborough: Saxon House.

Mirrlees-Black, C. (1993) *Disqualification from Driving: an Effective Penalty?* Home Office Research and Planning Unit Paper 74. London: Home Office.

Office for National Statistics (2000) *Social Trends 30* London: The Stationery Office.

Ogilivie-Smith, A., Downey, A. and Ransom, E. (1994) *Traffic Policing: Activity and Organisation.* Police Research Series No. 12. London: Home Office.

Riley, D. (1985) 'Drinking drivers: the limits to deterrence' *The Howard Journal.* 24: 241-256.

Russell, J. (1998) *Phoenix Data Quality.* Police Research Group Special Series. London: Home Office.

Smerdon, J. and South N. (1997) 'Deviant drivers and 'moral hazards': risk, no-insurance offending, and some suggestions for policy and practice' *International Journal of Risk, Security and Crime Prevention.* 2(4): 279-290.

Steer, D.J. and Carr-Hill, R.A. (1967) 'The motoring offender - who is he?' *Criminal Law Review.* 1967: 214-224.

Sugg, D. (1998) *Motor Projects in England and Wales: a Evaluation.* Home Office Research, Development and Statistics Directorate, Research Findings No. 81. London: Home Office.

Walker, N. and Hough, M. (1998) 'Schools for crime — dangerous drivers after imprisonment' *New Law Journal.* July 24 1998.

West Midlands Police (1997) *Annual Report.* Http://www.webworld.net

Willett, T.C. (1964) *Criminal on the Road: a Study of Serious Motoring Offences and those who commit them.* London: Tavistock.

Wolf, P. (1964) "The Myth of the Respectable Traffic Offender" *Sociologiske Meddelelser,* 1:73-77.

Notes

RDS Publications

Requests for Publications

Copies of our publications and a list of those currently available may be obtained from:

Home Office
Research, Development and Statistics Directorate
Communications Development Unit
Room 201, Home Office
50 Queen Anne's Gate
London SW1H 9AT
Telephone: 020 7273 2084 (answerphone outside of office hours)
Facsimile: 020 7222 0211
E-mail: publications.rds@homeoffice.gsi.gov.uk

alternatively

why not visit the RDS web-site at
          Internet: http://www.homeoffice.gov.uk/rds/index.htm

where many of our publications are availabe to be read on screen or downloaded for printing.